SOFT TOY MAKING

A History of Toys

A toy, broadly speaking, is any item that can be used for play – generally by children and pets. Toys and games are most frequently used (consciously or not) as an enjoyable means of training the young for life in society. The young use toys and play to discover their identity, help their bodies grow strong, learn cause and effect, explore relationships, and practice skills they will need as adults. Adults use toys and play to form and strengthen social bonds, teach, reinforce lessons from their youth, discover their identity, exercise their minds and bodies, explore relationships and decorate their living spaces. Many items are designed to serve as toys (often purely as collectors' items), but goods produced for other purposes can also be used. For instance, a small child may pick up a household item and "fly" it through the air as to pretend that it is an airplane. Today, another consideration is 'interactive digital entertainment' – a wholly novel development which is quickly changing the world of toys as we know it.

The origin of toys is prehistoric; dolls representing infants, animals, and soldiers, as well as representations of tools used by adults are readily found at archaeological sites. The origin of the word "toy" is unknown, but it is believed that it was first used in the fourteenth century. Toys excavated from the Indus valley civilization (3000-1500 BCE) include small carts, whistles shaped like birds, and toy monkeys which could slide down a string. All of these earliest toys are made from materials readily found in nature, such as rocks, sticks and clay. The first 'sophisticated' toys were found in Egypt – where children played with dolls that had wigs and movable limbs which were made from stone, pottery, and wood. In Ancient Greece and Ancient Rome, children played with dolls made of wax or terracotta, sticks, bows and arrows, and yo-yos. When Greek children, especially girls, came of age it was customary for them to sacrifice the toys of their childhood to the gods. On the eve of their wedding, young girls around fourteen would offer their dolls in a temple as a rite of passage into adulthood.

Toys, of course, do not merely involve dolls and replicas; they train the brain and the body as well as the imagination. The oldest known mechanical puzzle also comes from Greece and appeared in the Third century BC, it consists of a square divided into fourteen parts, and the aim was to create different shapes from these pieces. In Iran "puzzle-locks" were made as early as the seventeenth century AD. Such examples are anomalies though, and before the enlightenment era, toys were a rarity. This changed with novel attitudes towards children; seeing them as people in and of themselves, as opposed to extensions of their household. This prompted the school of thought that children had a right to flourish and enjoy their childhood. Consequently, the variety and number of toys that were manufactured during the eighteenth century steadily rose. John Spilsbury invented the first jigsaw puzzle in 1767 to help children learn geography and the rocking horse (on bow rockers) was also developed at the same time in England, especially for the wealthy as it was thought to develop children's balance for riding real horses. The first board games were produced by John Jefferys in the 1750s, including *A Journey Through Europe*. The game was very similar to modern board games, with players moving along a track with the throw of a dice (a teetotum was actually used) and landing on different spaces would either help or hinder the player.

In the nineteenth century, the emphasis was put on toys that had an educational purpose to them, such as puzzles, books, cards and board games. Religiously themed toys were also popular, including a model Noah's Ark with miniature animals and objects from other Bible scenes. With growing prosperity among the middle class, children also had more leisure time on their hands, which led to the application of industrial methods to the manufacture of toys. More complex mechanical and optics-based toys were also invented. Carpenter and Westley began to mass-produce the kaleidoscope, invented by Sir David Brewster in 1817, and had sold over 200,000 items within three months in London and Paris. The company was also able to mass-produce magic lanterns for use in phantasmagoria and galanty shows, by developing a method of mass production using a copper plate printing process. Popular imagery on the lanterns included royalty, flora and fauna, and geographical/man-made structures from around the world.

Despite these impressive developments, the golden age of toy development was at the turn of the twentieth century. Real wages were rising steadily in the Western world, allowing even working-class families to afford toys for their children, and industrial techniques of precision engineering and mass production was able to provide the supply to meet this rising demand. Intellectual emphasis was also increasingly being placed on the importance of a wholesome and happy childhood for the future development of children. William Harbutt, an English painter, invented plasticine in 1897, and in 1900 commercial production of the material as a children's toy began. Frank Hornby was a visionary in toy development and manufacture and was responsible for the invention and production of three of the most popular lines of toys based on engineering principles in the twentieth century: Meccano, Hornby Model Railways and Dinky Toys. During the Second World War, some new types of toys were created through accidental innovation. After trying to create a replacement for synthetic rubber, the American Earl L. Warrick inadvertently invented "nutty putty" during World War II. Later, Peter Hodgson recognized the potential as a childhood plaything and packaged it as Silly Putty. In 1943, at the height of the war, Richard James was experimenting with springs as part of his military research when he saw one come loose and fall to the floor. He was intrigued by the way it flopped around on the floor – and the result became the "Slinky".

After the Second World War, as society became ever more affluent and new technology and materials (plastics) for toy manufacture became available, toys became cheap and ubiquitous in households across the Western World. Among the more well-known products of the 1950s there was the Danish company Lego's line of colourful interlocking plastic brick construction sets, Rubik's Cube, the Barbie doll and Action Man. Today there are computerized dolls that can recognize and identify objects, the voice of their owner, and choose among hundreds of pre-programmed phrases with which to respond. The materials that toys are made from have changed, what toys can do has changed, but their appeal has not. We hope the reader enjoys this book.

SOME OF THE TOYS DESCRIBED IN THIS BOOK

Frontispiece

SOFT TOY MAKING

BY

OUIDA PEARSE, A.M.C.

HEAD OF NEEDLEWORK DEPARTMENT, PLYMOUTH
SCHOOL OF ARTS AND CRAFTS

PREFACE

For many years Soft Toy Making has been a favourite home occupation, and during the last few years especially the interest in this form of craft has been remarkably keen.

The models described in this book are such as usually appeal to the young. The instructions for their making have been given in such close detail that the craft worker should be able to carry them out without difficulty.

A set of full size patterns has been prepared for the guidance of the worker. The drawings may be used in several ways, but the intention in any case is that the material to be used shall be cut exactly to the size of the drawings. This supplement is published separately, at the price of 2s. net.

O. P.

CONTENTS

ILLUSTRATIONS

COLOUR

Some of the Toys Described in this Book   .   *Frontispiece*

BLACK AND WHITE

ILLUSTRATIONS

SOFT TOY MAKING

CHAPTER I

INTRODUCTORY

FROM the very earliest times men, women, and children
have made toys; the craft of Toy Making has this
advantage over other crafts in that toys have almost
always been made for the pure love of making them or
for some much-loved child, so that their production has
called forth the very best that is in the producer.

Soft toys seem to have been most made during the
last fifty years, and they may be ranked among the
most popular of modern toys. Taking a glance at the
toys which remain to us in museums dolls are best
represented, but there are not many rag or "soft" ones.
It may be that stuffed toys have been made, but not
being as durable as those of wood and other materials,
few have come down to us, and animals and other toys
are nearly always made of wood, bone, metal, or some
fairly hard substance. One of the most delightful of the
ancient animals is the lion in a case in the fourth
Egyptian Room, British Museum. It is carved in
wood, and has a movable lower jaw which can be
worked up and down by pulling a string which passes
up through the top of its head.

While in the same museum, in the Greek and Roman
Life Room, is a rag doll, third century A.D. It is made
of coarse linen and is very dilapidated. The body and

1

head seem to be sewn into a shape and stuffed with rag, and the arms and legs are rolls of linen.

In this little book it is hoped to indicate methods and ideas for soft toy making which will be useful in the *Home*. For a hand-made toy possesses more character and is far more durable than most shop toys, besides the pleasure which will be got from making it.

In *schools* soft toy making, besides being a craft which calls forth every faculty, can also be made a useful aid to study.

HISTORY. If a class of girls studying a certain period in history made a set of dolls and dressed them in the costume of that period, their work would have a wonderful meaning and reality. This need not give a lot of work to the teacher, as the reference libraries have excellent books on costume (one of the best being *Costume and Fashion*, by Herbert Morris, in two volumes), and the girls can go and search out the style of costume for themselves. Neither need it be expensive, as the dolls may be as simple in type as those in the Girl Doll "Jane," Chapter III.

A useful thing for any school to have would be a set of dolls dressed in the main periods of English costume : Anglo-Saxon, Norman, Early English, etc.

LITERATURE. The making of puppets and puppet shows as described at the beginning of Chapter VII. There is a great deal of pleasure and instruction to be had from designing, making, and manipulating puppets.

GEOGRAPHY. A class studying a foreign country might well make a set of animals of that country. These could be quite simple, like the silhouettes in Chapter IV, or more realistic like the animals in

Chapter VI. Again, a doll in the costume of the country would help.

DRESS DESIGN. Dolls of the slender type shown in Chapter VIII are very useful for those practising dress design. New styles and colour schemes can be very easily and cheaply tried on them. While the use of one or two of these in the sewing classes of schools would do a great deal to stimulate the interest of the girls.

TOYS FOR SALE. In women's and girls' clubs, Girl Guide companies, and women's institutes, toys will be found the most saleable articles if funds are required. A toy stall which held all the toys in this book, some of them many times repeated in different colouring and materials, would prove a very attractive part of a sale or exhibition.

GENERAL INSTRUCTIONS AND IMPORTANT POINTS ABOUT SOFT TOY MAKING

CHOICE OF MATERIAL. Almost any material can be used. For dolls a fine underclothing material or fugi is best—avoid fabrics both for dolls and animals which are loosely woven, avoid artificial silks except, of course, for the clothing of dolls. Animal baize of all kinds which will give a most realistic appearance to animals can be obtained—this is used for dog Toby, Plate XVII, but this material is rather expensive and more difficult to use than smooth material.

Toy making is a good way of using up the sound parts of worn-out garments. Parts of men's suits will make very good toys. The garments should always be ripped or cut up, washed in lux, and pressed before use. The grey donkey, Plate XVI, can be most successfully made from a pair of grey flannel trousers. Even if the whole of each part of the pattern cannot be cut in one piece—a join which is well pressed hardly shows.

THE PATTERN AND METHOD OF CUTTING OUT. It is impossible to attach too much importance to nicety of pattern and care in cutting out material. The pattern should always be firmly held or pinned on to the wrong side of stuff and an accurate outline painted, with Chinese white if the material is dark and with black paint if it is light. The necessary turnings are then allowed for outside this painted line, the toy is tacked together and the sewing done exactly on the painted line.

The first mistake made by most amateur toy makers is to pin the pattern on material as in dressmaking, cut it out—often most inaccurately—before removing it and stitching.

They then expect the toy to have all the nicety of contour of a toy which has been made with a carefully drawn outline, and are surprised when it does not look like the illustration they are copying.

SEWING SEAMS. Use silk substitute in a matching colour. Toys must always be firmly and accurately tacked. There are four ways of sewing seams for toys : (1) Backstitching on the wrong side by hand; (2) Oversewing on cut edges without turning; (3) Machining on right side, allowing about $\frac{1}{8}$ in. turning, which is cut on right side (these last two methods can only be used on felt or material which will not fray); (4) Machining on wrong side.

Machining is better than hand sewing if the machinist is expert and can exactly follow the painted line—if she is not, it is far better to backstitch by hand. All toy making by children is best done by hand.

STUFFING. Kapok for the smaller toys and dolls, and wood wool for the more elaborate and jointed toys is best. If expense is an important consideration other things can be used. Rags picked into small pieces will do, but they are apt to be lumpy, however careful the worker is, and the slightly modelled effect which is such an important feature of a successful soft toy cannot be obtained as with Kapok. Sheep's wool, if it can be gathered by children in the country, is very good for stuffing—it must be washed and dried.

The way a toy is stuffed is important. The stuffing *must* be put in small pieces, each pushed firmly down before the next is added (a wooden meat skewer may be used for this pushing) and the toy, whether stuffed with Kapok or wood wool, should feel very firm when new, as the stuffing shakes down with use and the toy becomes softer.

PUTTING IN EYES. For the simpler toys eyes can be put in with stitches, but glass eyes give a very realistic effect to the more elaborate toys. These eyes are sold attached to each end of a wire. To put in cut the wire in half, shorten to about 1 in. behind each eye, put the eye in position, push the wire through the material so that 1 in. is on the wrong side, curl this wire into a loop with pliers and press it against the back of the eye, so that the eye is held tightly in position.

TREATMENT OF DOLL'S HAIR. Sheep's wool makes the best fair and brown hair, and cable rug wool the best black. To prepare the sheep's wool take it direct from the fleece and wash it well in lux. On several of the dolls described in this book the sheep's wool is used white, and it is very beautiful in effect that way. It can be turned slightly yellow by dipping it in strong cold tea. If golden and brown hair is required, dip the wool while it is wet (after washing it in lux) in Batik dye—dilute the dye according to the directions as for material. The Turkey rug wool has to be pulled abroad and combed. If very straight silky hair is required stranded cotton may be used.

DETAIL AND FINISH. Great care must be taken with these, and, generally speaking, it is best to put in eyes and face markings before the toy is stuffed, and in some cases while it is flat before being made up. These markings and finishings allow great scope for the individual taste and skill of the worker, and the whole character of a toy can be changed by the angle of an ear or the curl of a tail.

ENLARGING AND DECREASING SIZE OF PATTERNS. The patterns of toys given with this book are all of medium size, but if larger or smaller toys are required it is quite easy to enlarge or diminish a pattern. If the pattern of Toby dog (Plate XVII) is required half as large again, cut it out and lay it on paper ruled in 1 in. squares. Draw around it and remove it. (Fig. 1A.) Now rule a piece of paper in 1½ in. squares, copy the pattern from Fig. 1A, simply making its lines intersect the lines of the squares on the large pattern as they did on the small. (Fig. 1B.)

To decrease a pattern simply lessen the size of the squares in the new pattern as required.

COST OF TOYS. This is mentioned in connection with each toy in this book, but it is only approximate, as much depends on whether odd lengths of wool, etc., can be used—if whole skeins have to be bought where only a needleful is required for marking purposes the cost is greatly increased.

Fig. 1b

Fig. 1a

SPECIAL MATERIALS. There are not many special materials used, but for the more elaborate toys one or two are essential, such as eyes, animal baize, felt, joints, and sheep's wool. These can all be procured from any of the well-known handicraft firms who will send most comprehensive catalogues and price lists on application. In many country districts sheep's wool can be collected from the hedges in the fields where sheep are kept, or any farmer will, as a rule, sell for a few pence a ½ lb., which will go a long way.

CHAPTER II

VERY SIMPLE TOYS

Come, ducklings so yellow;
Come, chicken so small,
Each soft little fellow
That can't run at all.

By Bjoïnstgerme Bjoïnson.

ALL who wish to make toys are not experts either as needle-women or in the manipulation of material, and the making of the more elaborate type of toy takes a good deal of skill. So in this chapter four very simple toys are described—there are no complex shapes or difficult parts to stuff, yet by their very simplicity these toys possess a great charm.

BUNNY RABBIT. (Plate IA.)

Materials—
White ripple cloth as used for dressing gowns.
¼ yd. of material 36 in. wide will make two rabbits.
Black mending wool.
Small piece of stiff cardboard.
Fairly large needle and cream silk.
Cost per rabbit 6d. to 8d.

Cut out pieces 1, 2, 3, 4, 5 from Pattern Sheet B, fold ripple cloth in two, wrong side out, lay down pattern as in Fig. 1c, and mark the outline carefully (this is best done with a fine brush and brown paint); now cut out in double material, leaving ¼ in. turnings. It will

9

be noted that four pieces are required for the ear and four for the feet.

Some of the toys described later may be machined, but this one is best made by hand. Backstitch body, head, and tail circles on the painted outline, pull the stitches rather tight to contract the edge of the circle,

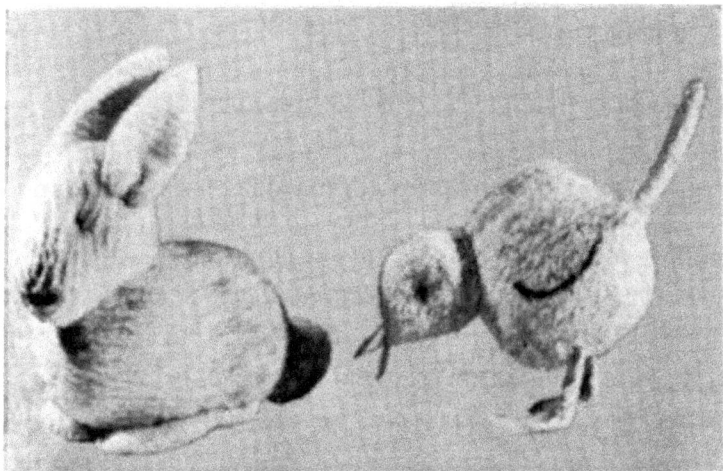

PLATE IA   PLATE IB
BUNNY RABBIT   CHICKEN

and leaving the part between the crosses open for stuffing.

Stuff the body with Kapok, stretch the circles into an oval, turn rather large turnings, and sew up between crosses. The ripple cloth, being easily stretched, will go readily into the oval-shaped body of the rabbit. (Fig. 2.)

Stuff the head and tail, again pressing them into slightly oval shapes, and turning large turnings, place them on the body and hem them in position with invisible stitches, the head between AB and the tail

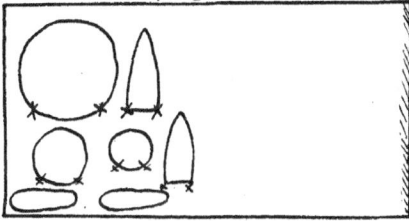

Fig 1 C

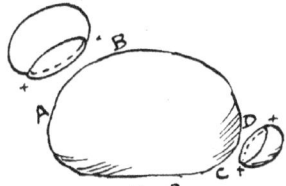

Fig 2

Fig 3. B

Fig3.C.

Fig 3. A

Fig 3. D.

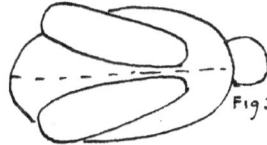

Fig 3. E

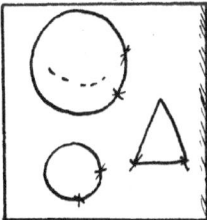

Fig 4. A

Fig 4 B

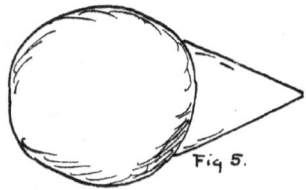

Fig 5.

Fig 6. A

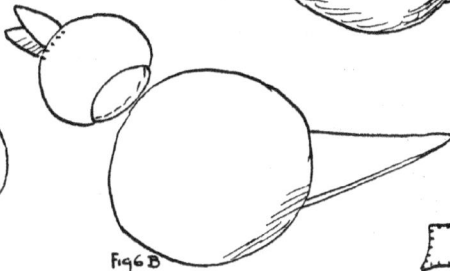

Fig 6 B

Fig 6. C

between *CD*, Fig. 2. Backstitch the ears, leaving open between crosses for turning right side out. Fig. 3 shows, *A*, the sides of the ear folded over; *B*, the ear turned back and stitched; *C*, the ear turned up and sewn to the head at the back, and the position of the eye, which is made with several backstitches in black wool; *D* shows three black wool backstitches for the nose.

A slightly modelled effect is given to the head if the needle is passed forwards and backwards from eye to eye and pulled tight.

Cut two pieces of cardboard as Pattern Piece 5, Sheet A, for the feet, tack feet pieces on each side of cardboard, turn ripple cloth edge to edge and oversew all around. Place feet in position as *E*, Fig. 3 (which shows underpart of rabbit), and sew firmly in place.

CHICKEN. (Plate IB.)

Materials—

White Turkey towelling ¼ yd. of 18 in.
Piece of stiff cardboard.
Small piece of white calico.
Black wool, white cotton.

Cut out pattern pieces 6, 7, 8, 9, 10, Sheet A, and place body, head, and tail on material folded double (Fig. 4A). Place legs and beak on calico folded double Fig. 4B), mark around and cut out as for rabbit. Backstitch body, head, and tail on outline and turn right side out. Cut cardboard as for tail, legs, and beak, push cardboard between tail pieces and sew up between crosses. Stuff body, place tail between crosses, and sew, slightly flattening body circle to receive tail, Fig. 5 shows top view. Place calico on each side of beak pieces (there should be two cardboard beaks and four

pieces of calico), tack in place, turn calico edge to edge
and oversew around legs and feet in the same way.
Push two beaks between part of head marked *O–O*, and
sew in position before head is stuffed. Stuff head and
hem in place (Fig. 6B). Bend feet at dotted line so that
they look like Fig. 6c, and sew firmly in position so that
the chicken will stand. Mark wings in black wool and
backstitch them and the eyes with several backstitches.

The chicken looks very well in white as described,
but if desired the towelling may be dyed yellow
and flesh-coloured casement cloth used for feet and
beak.

SPOTTED DUCK. (Plate II.)

    Materials—

        $\frac{1}{4}$ yd. of spotted print, 36 in. will make two ducks.

        Small piece of orange felt.

        Small piece of cardboard.

        Pair of duck's eyes.

        Kapok for stuffing.

Soft toys made of patterned prints are very attractive and very cheap, but it is important that the
pattern should exactly suit the particular toy. For
instance, a duck made of either a flowered or a plaid
material would not look well. Fig. 7 gives an idea of a
suitable pattern, it may be any colour.

Cut out pieces 11, 12, 13, 14, and 15 from Pattern
Sheet A. Cut $\frac{1}{4}$ yd. of print into two pieces each 18 in.
by 9 in., fold one of these in half and place body, chest,
and wing on double material, folding chest pattern at
dotted line. Fig. 8 shows pattern laid out. Paint outline and cut out, leaving $\frac{1}{4}$ in. turnings. Cut out beak
and feet in double felt, and feet in single cardboard.

Print toys are best machined, as the machine makes a more even seam than hand sewing. Tack duck together, placing chest piece so that letters *A*, *B*, *C* correspond, and leaving opening between crosses for stuffing.

Backstitch beak on right side as in Fig. 9A and

PLATE II
SPOTTED DUCK

oversew feet, placing cardboard between two pieces of felt (Fig. 10B). Put in eyes of duck (see general instructions). Stuff with Kapok and sew up; stuff wings a little and sew in position as indicated on pattern. Stuff beak and oversew on to opening *O--O*, as in Fig. 10A. Sew on feet as in Fig. 10C, which shows underpart of duck.

Soft Ball. (Plate III.)

Materials—

Six pieces of different coloured materials; felt is best.
　　Kapok for stuffing.

Cost—

　　The smallest amount of felt that can be pur-
　　chased is ⅛ yd. of each colour. ⅝ yd. cost 3s.,
　　and will make ten balls, so the cost per ball
　　with the stuffing would be about 6d.

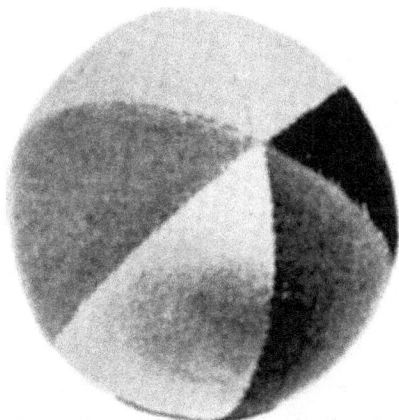

Plate III
Soft Ball

These balls make a fine patch of colour arranged in a
flat basket or in a pile on a stall, and sell well as a rule.
Cut out pattern 16 on Sheet A, lay on felt and mark
carefully around with chalk on six different coloured
pieces. Oversew on wrong side (see Fig. 11), leaving a
space for stuffing between crosses on two pieces. Stuff
and sew up.

This ball can also be made of casement cloth or odd

pieces of material—these pieces must be cut with a
$\frac{1}{4}$ in. turning, the shape of the pattern having first
been carefully marked out with paint—it is best to
oversew balls on the right side. If made this way the
stitches improve the look of the ball, and it is easy to
get the pieces to fit, but if sewn from the wrong side
it is very difficult when turnings are taken to get the
six sections to meet exactly at the ends.

CHAPTER III

No! No! let us play for it is yet day
And we cannot go to sleep.
Besides in the sky the little birds fly
And the hills are all covered with sheep.

WILLIAM BLAKE.

MANY delightful toys for small children can be made with simple tubular or sausage shapes of different sizes and lengths. Patterns and instructions for the making of four toys are given, but it will be found that very good results can be obtained by experimenting without any patterns.

To begin, get some cheap material in bright colours, cut strips of different widths, one perhaps 5 in. wide and about 18 in. long, another 2½ in. wide and 1 yd. long, another 3½ in. wide and 1 yd. long. Fold the strips with the long edges together and machine on the wrong side; now turn right side out and stuff the long tubular pieces. The 5 in. strips will make bodies, the intermediate strips legs, and small pieces arms, simply cut them in lengths as required, neatly sew up the ends, either gathering them or oversewing them square, then sew legs and arms on to bodies as required.

The way to add heads, hands, and feet will be shown in the two toys which follow.

Another way of using the tubes or sausage shapes is simply to add a shaped animal's head—these are particularly suitable for small children, as they are so light and easy to hold.

17

BOY DOLL—" BILL." (Plate IV.)

Materials—

$\frac{1}{8}$ yd. of green casement cloth.

$\frac{1}{8}$ yd. of yellow casement cloth.

Small piece of flesh-coloured casement cloth.

Small piece of black casement cloth.

Small piece of black felt.

1 yd. of black cable rug wool.

Black and red paint.

Kapok to stuff.

Cost 9d.

Cut out pieces 1, 2, 3, 4, 5, 6, 7, 8, and 9 from Sheet B. Cut each $\frac{1}{8}$ yd. of casement into two pieces 18 in. by $4\frac{1}{2}$ in. Take a piece of yellow and a piece of green, fold as in Fig. 12, and lay down and cut out pattern pieces 1 and 2 on each colour, allowing $\frac{1}{4}$ in. turning on one side. Cut out two pieces, as in pattern 3, in black casement cloth for feet. Machine on wrong side and turn out to right side. Gather bottom of legs and sew up, stuff feet and sew up (they should look like little oblong bags). Sew them to bottom of leg. (Fig. 13A.) Stuff legs and gather tops and sew up. Now over-sew two tubular legs together (Fig. 13B) and, using strong thread and a darning needle pull the stitches tight, so that they sink into the stuffing and become invisible. Cut out two head pieces and two hand pieces in flesh-coloured casement cloth. Gather hand pieces all round and draw up and stuff so that they are like small balls. Turn in edge of arm tubes at bottom and hem balls in to form hands. (Fig. 13c.) Stuff arm, turn in top diagonally, and hem on (Fig. 13B.) Paint face, place head pieces right sides together and stitch;

PLATE IV
BOY DOLL "BILL"

turn right side out, gather slightly between crosses, and
stuff; sew neatly on to top of body tubes. (Fig. 13B.)

Pull out the wrinkles in the rug wool and sew on all
over head. Cut out collar in two thicknesses of green

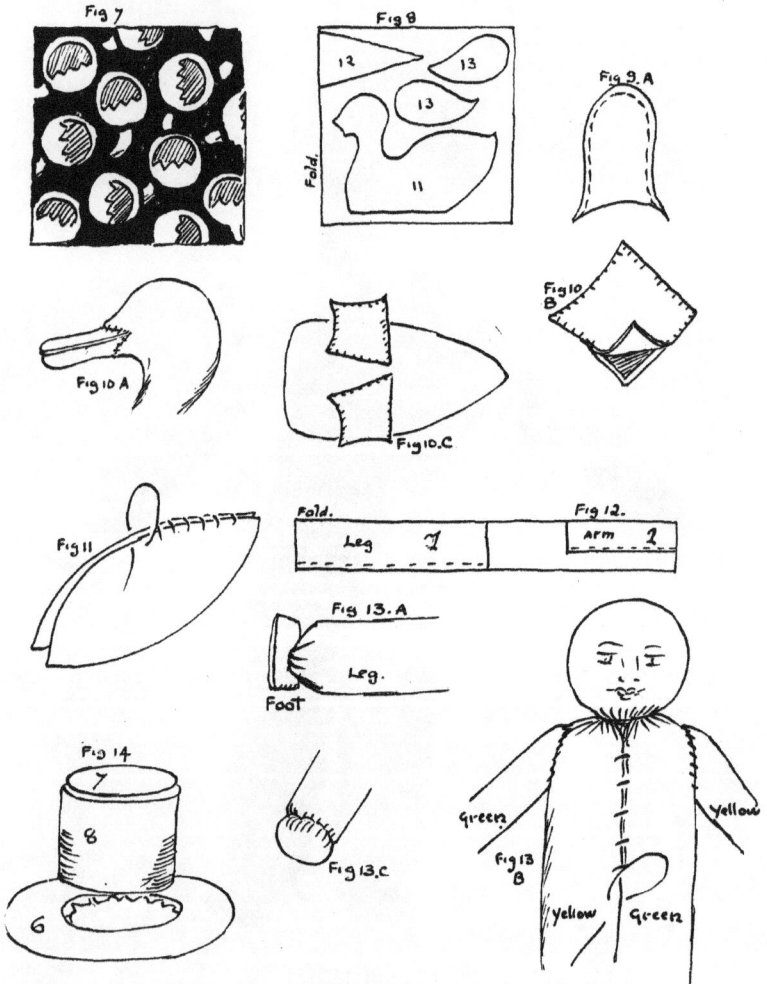

casement cloth. Machine on wrong side and turn to right, turn neck edge to edge and slipstitch on collar. (Plate IV.)

Fig. 14 shows hat pieces 6, 7, 8 from Pattern Sheet B in position ready to be sewn together. Pieces 6 and 8 should first be cut in cardboard. Pattern 8 is only half the length of piece, the part between crosses must be doubled. The brim must be covered with yellow casement cloth underneath and green above—to do this, tack two circles of material above and below cardboard, allowing turnings at edge. Turn in edges and oversew around : do the same at head opening, snipping material as shown in Fig. 14.

Sew crown into position and cover with yellow casement. Then put in green top to crown, which need not be stiffened with cardboard. Sew hat firmly on to doll ; cut disks of black felt about the size of threepenny bits, and sew them in position like buttons between tubes on body and on collar and hat as shown in Plate IV.

GIRL DOLL—"JANE." (Plate V.)

Materials—

¼ yd. of black casement cloth.
¼ yd. of orange casement cloth.
Small piece of cardboard.
10 small orange wooden beads.
Some sheep's wool or cream-coloured rug wool.
Small piece of flesh-coloured casement cloth.
Black and red paint.
Kapok for stuffing.
Cost 10d.

Cut out pieces 2, 3, 4, 10, and 11 from Pattern Sheet B. The body, one arm, leg, and foot are black, also the hat and bodice of dress and one hand frill.

Cut ¼ yd. of black casement into two pieces each 18 in. by 9 in., fold one piece in half, place pieces 10, 2, and 3, and extend piece 2 for 6½ in. to form leg. (Fig. 15A.) Cut ¼ yd. of orange casement cloth in the

PLATE V
GIRL DOLL "JANE"

same way and arrange pieces 2 and 3 and leg piece. (Fig. 15B.) Cut out, allowing ¼ in. turnings, and machine these pieces to form tubes, except feet and body, which may have one short end machined across. Cut out head and hands in flesh-coloured casement cloth. Paint face. Stuff head and body and fix on head. Stuff feet and legs and fix on feet. Make and stuff hands and fix in place. Stuff arms and attach to body as described for the boy doll "Bill." (Figs. 13A, 13B, and 13C.) Turn in tops of legs and oversew (Fig. 16A), oversew legs to bottom of body (which should be like an oblong bag). (Fig. 16B.)

Dressing of "Jane." She simply wears a tight bodice of black, a pleated skirt of orange, an orange frill at neck and on her black arm, and a black frill on her orange arm. On her head a black pointed hat.

The skirt is a straight piece of material 24 in. by 4½ in. It can be cut from the other piece of orange casement cloth which is 18 in. by 9 in. by cutting this into two strips each 18 in. by 4½ in. and cutting 12 in. lengths off each. The bottom of the skirt should be cut in scallops, the shape of which can be marked out from pattern piece 12, Sheet B. The scallops may be button-holed or left the raw edge of material.

Join skirt at sides and sew in even pleats around waist of doll. The black bodice of dress is a straight piece 6½ in. by 3 in. The top and bottom and front edge of this piece are folded (Fig. 17A), sewn on to doll, and then taken over top of pleats of skirt (Fig. 17B) and neatly sewn up the front, on which five orange beads are sewn as buttons.

The hand frills are strips 6½ in. by 1¾ in. which are joined and arranged in pleats around hands.

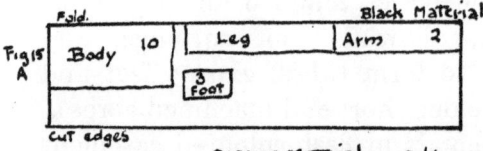

Fold. Black Material

Fig 15 A

Body 10   Leg   Arm 2

3 Foot

cut edges

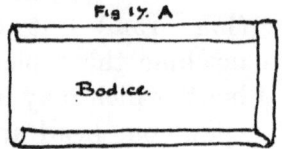

Fig 17. A

Bodice.

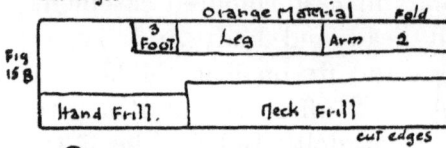

Orange Material   Fold

Fig 15 B

3 Foot   Leg   Arm 2

Hand Frill.   Neck Frill

cut edges

Fig 16 A

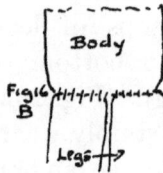

Body

Fig 16 B

Legs

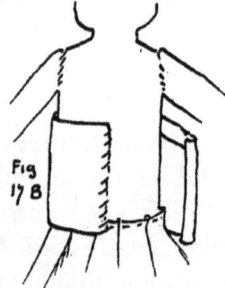

Fig 17 B

Fig 18 A.

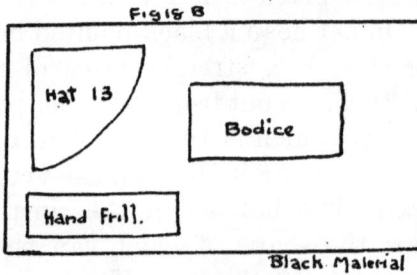

Fig 18 B

Hat 13

Bodice

Hand Frill.

Black Material

Fig 19.

Fig 20. A.

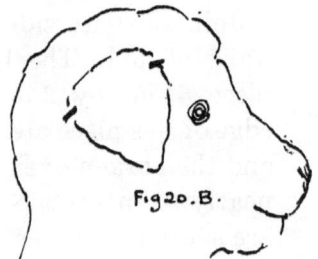

Fig 20. B.

Fig 20. C.

The neck frill is 11½ in. by 2 in., and is just pleated around neck.

The sheep's wool or rug wool is arranged as short hair. The hat is made from pattern piece 13, Sheet B, which is cut in cardboard and covered with black casement cloth, the join of both cardboard and material being in front with a row of orange beads to hide it. (Fig. 18A.) Sew hat firmly on to doll. Fig. 18B shows hat, bodice, and hand frill placed on remaining half of black casement cloth.

TIBBY LAMB TOY. (Plate VIA.)

Materials—
¼ yd. of curly animal baize, 50 in. wide, will make four toys.
Pair of small brown eyes.
½ yd. of jade green corded ribbon.
Three brass bells.
Black mending wool.
Cost 1s.

Cut out pieces 14, 15, 16, and 17 from Pattern Sheet B. Lay pieces on wrong side of baize and paint around. Mark position of eyes. (Fig. 19.) Cut out, leaving ¼ in. turnings.

Put in eyes, tack parts together (letters correspond in fitting in forehead piece). Machine or backstitch by hand on wrong side and turn to right side. Stuff from bottom and hem in base piece.

Make ears—each has two pieces which should be placed right side to right side, stitched around and turned out. Sew ears in position (Figs. 20A and 20B), and mark nose and mouth in wool back stitch. (Fig. 20C.)

The stitches shown in Fig. 20B, although they are needed to make the ear turn down, should sink into the baize and become invisible.

Tie ribbon around neck with the three bells in front and bow at back, which should be firmly sewn to keep it from untying.

NEDDY THE DONKEY. (Plate VIB.)

> Materials—
>
>   ¼ yd. of 36 in. grey felt will make two donkeys.
>   Small pieces of black, red, and yellow felt.
>   Grey silko.
>   Pair of small brown eyes.
>   Kapok for stuffing.

Cut out pieces 17, 18, 19, and 20, Pattern Sheet B. Cut ¼ yd. of felt into two pieces each 18 in. by 9 in. Fold one piece in half, lay out pattern, and mark around. (Fig. 21.)

Cut out, leaving NO turnings, put in eye and mark the position of nostril, mouth, eyebrow, and ear-slit with chalk. Cut out these details in black felt and sew eyebrow and nostril in position with grey backstitch as in Figs. 22A and 22B.

Make ears, each ear being made from two pieces of felt oversewn together at edge on right side. Cut slit for ears as in A and B, pattern piece 18, Sheet B. Fold ears, insert them in slit and hem in place. (See Fig. 22C.)

Oversew forehead piece in position from right side, making C and D pattern pieces 18 and 20 fit.

Now oversew all of donkey together except part between F and D. Cut a strip of felt 7 in. by 1½ in., shape it like a fringe as in Fig. 23A, cut through forehead piece on dotted line D to E, and insert fringed

PLATE VIB
NEDDY THE DONKEY

PLATE VIA
TIBBY LAMB TOY

piece of felt for donkey's mane. Stitch in position and cut several longer fringed pieces and sew to hang down over donkey's eyes. Stuff from bottom and hem in base.

Backstitch mouthpiece of black felt in position as in Fig. 23c.

Cut ½ in. strip of red felt for collar, sew on and ornament with two yellow squares at back of neck.

If the donkey will squeak it adds to its interest for a small child. The squeaker must be of the kind which makes a noise by pressing, and must also be small. These can generally be obtained at toy and novelty shops. To put in: When the neck of donkey is about half stuffed, insert the squeaker, stuff around it, leaving sufficient room for the pressure, and sew up opening.

CHAPTER IV

SILHOUETTE TOYS

Clowns that laugh
And elves that play.

THIS chapter still deals with toys which are very simple and cheap to make, in some ways easier than those already described, except that a little more care will be required in the stuffing of the extremities, such as hands and feet of figures and legs and tails of animals. It is surprising what good results can be obtained by copying the silhouette of a distinctive type of figure or animal, slightly thickening the parts, such as necks and legs, then cutting out the silhouette in two thicknesses of material, sewing accurate outlines, and stuffing.

MAD HARE. (Plate VIIA.)
  Materials—
    ¼ yd. of 36 in. yellow casement cloth.
    1d. skein of red wool.
    1d. skein of stranded blue cotton.
    Kapok to stuff.
    Cost 7d.

Cut out pattern pieces 1 and 2 from Sheet C, fold ¼ yd. of casement cloth so that it makes a double rectangle 18 in. by 9 in., lay down pattern pieces 1 and 2 (Fig. 23), and paint outline but not inner markings. Cut out, allowing turnings. Machine or sew accurately the outline on wrong side, and before turning to right

Top—PLATE VIIA   *Bottom*—PLATE VIIB
MAD HARE   GIDDY ELEPHANT

side snip all corners, such as that between leg and body. Fig. 24A shows corner X with the snips made.

Also cut off tips of sharp points such as tail and mouth. Fig. 24B shows this done at mouth, the cuts being shown in checked lines. Leave part between O–O open for stuffing. Turn right side out, being careful to well press out all points and curves, as all the charm of this type of toy depends on the drawing of the outline.

Now lay hare flat on a board or table and fit on pattern. With a piece of carbon paper between it and the pattern trace over markings on both sides, using dotted lines in connection with tops of legs for one side and black lines for the other.

Couch cable wool (red) on every part of outline which has been traced, using three strands of blue embroidery cotton for couching stitches; Fig. 25A shows this being done. Stitch eyes with several back- · stitches one over the other, taking stitches right through head and pulling tight to give modelling. Make ears, each ear being made of two pieces of casement cloth with stiff paper between. Cut paper a little smaller then material, and turn material edge to edge over paper. Tack and couch red line around edge. Fig. 25B shows ear with point turned back showing paper stiffening in shaded lines and turnings of yellow material on other side of ear. Sew on ear in the way described for the rabbit's ear. (Figs. 3A, 3B, 3C, p. 11.) Paint in markings in blue paint, using paint very dry or it will run.

The mad hare just described is quickly made and costs very little. It may, however, be made in yellow felt with the markings worked in wool backstitch, or in linen with the markings worked in coloured cotton.

GIDDY ELEPHANT. (Plate VIIB)

Materials—
    ⅜ yd. of 36 in. blue casement cloth.
    Skein of yellow anchor flox.
    Skein of black stranded cotton.
    Small piece of galvanized wire.
    Kapok.
    Cost 9d.

Cut out pattern pieces 3 and 4, Sheet C. Fig. 26A shows material folded in half and pattern laid out. The elephant is made in exactly the same way as the hare, except that anchor flox is used for the outline instead of wool, and the tail is made separately, wired, and attached.

Complete elephant, all but the couched outline, then sew tail and turn right side out. Cut a piece of wire about 3½ in. long, bend ends into small loops (Fig. 26B), and bind with kapok until it is just large enough to push into tail. Fig. 27 shows tail as if it were transparent with wire inside. Sew on tail, making *AB* on tail correspond to *AB* on elephant. Complete elephant, using black for couching on the yellow outline.

LITTLE ELF DOLL. (Plate VIIIA.)

Materials—

¼ yd. of 36 in. orange felt will make two dolls.
Small piece of white felt.
Small piece of black felt.
Kapok.
Cost 9d.

Cut out pattern pieces 5, 6, 7, and 8, Sheet C. Cut ¼ yd. of felt into two rectangles 18 in. by 9 in., and fold one of these in half so that it makes a double 9 in. square. Lay No. 5 pattern on it, paint around and cut out, leaving NO turnings. Lay down pieces 6 and 7 on white felt and piece 8 on black, mark around and cut out in the same way. The features may be traced on to No. 6 piece with carbon paper. Place piece 6 in position behind opening *A* in the head of piece 5, hem orange edges of head over white face neatly. Either work face in black wool or paint it with black paint.

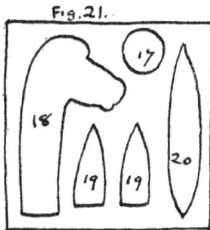

Fig. 21.

17

18

19 19 20

Fold.

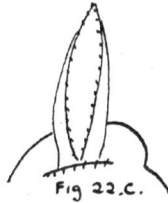

Fig. 22. A.

Fig 22 B

Fig 22. C.

Fig 23. B.

Fig 23. A.

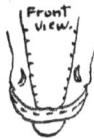

Front View.

Fig 23. C.

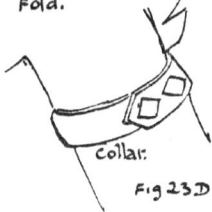

Collar.

Fig 23 D

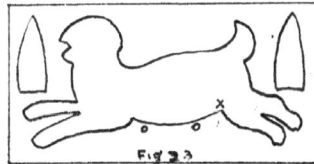

FOLD

Fig 23

Fig. 24. B.

X

Fig 24. A

Fig 25. A

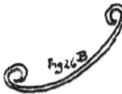

Fig 26 B

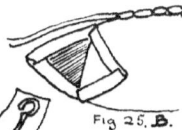

Fig 25. B.

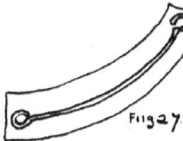

Fig 27

Fig 26. A.

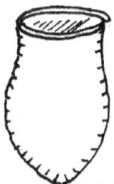

Fig 28 A

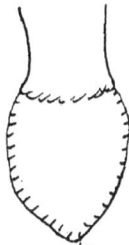

Fig 28 B

Fig 29 A

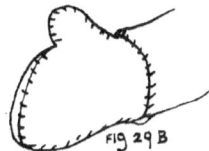

Fig 29 B

Neatly oversew edges of hands, feet, and body, leaving opening between crosses in each case for stuffing.

PLATE VIIIB
CLOWN DOLL

PLATE VIIIA
LITTLE ELF DOLL

There should be two pieces for each hand and two for each foot. Stuff heads and feet and fit into position so that seams match, arms overlap hands, and legs overlap feet to dotted lines on pattern pieces. Hem in hands and feet. Stuff whole of elf and sew up opening. Fig. 28A shows foot sewn and stuffed, Fig. 28B foot attached to leg, Figs. 29A and 29B hand stuffed and attached.

CLOWN DOLL. (Plate VIIIB.)

Materials—
$\frac{1}{2}$ yd. of 36 in. white felt.
Small piece of orange felt.
Small piece of black felt.
Black wool.
Kapok.
Cost 1s. 3d.

Cut out pattern piece 9, Sheet C. Pin single felt on a board or table, pin pattern down with carbon paper, between felt and pattern, trace all lines; turn pattern over, lay down again and trace. Fig. 30A shows pattern laid out.

Cut each piece singly, as the outline is then likely to be more accurate in this rather intricate silhouette. Trace the part of the pattern which is black on black felt twice, and that which is in shaded lines on orange felt twice, turning the pattern over for the second tracing, so that the sides will be reversed. Tack these pieces (viz. sleeves orange, waistcoat and BOOTS BLACK) in place, and hem on. Fig. 30 shows a black boot being hemmed on.

Now tack the two main pieces together right side out and work coral stitch (Fig. 31) all around double edge of felt to join—it forms a knotted stitch, and the knots should be about $\frac{1}{8}$ in. apart. Leave part between crosses open for stuffing. Work all outlines on both pieces with wool, backstitch, stuff, and sew up. Now take some double wool and work a stabbed running stitch on all inner outlines—right through from side to side of the toy. This should draw the outlines together, and let the parts between rise and give that padded effect noticeable in Plate VIIIB, like quilting.

BABY DOLL. (Plate IX.) This doll shows the silhouette clothed and the use of a manufactured mask for a face. These masks can be obtained at 3d. each, and although their use is apt to give rather a cheap shop-bought look to a toy and take away something of the charm of the "all hand-made," yet some may wish to use these shop-purchased faces.

Materials—
　　¼ yd. of flesh-coloured cotton material.
　　Mask of doll's face.
　　¼ yd. of blue ripple cloth.
　　Small piece of cream ripple cloth.
　　Two small orange wooden beads.
　　¼ yd. of narrow orange ribbon.
　　Kapok.
　　Cost 1s. 3d.

Trace pattern piece 10 *black outline* on to fresh paper and cut out. Lay on double cotton material, mark outline and cut out, allowing turnings. Tack two pieces together and machine on outline, leaving opening between crosses for stuffing. Snip all corners as for the hare. (Fig. 24A.) Turn right side out, stuff, and sew up opening. Sew face mask on to front of head. Fig. 32A shows this done.

Dressing Doll. Fold ¼ yd. of blue ripple cloth in half to form a double rectangle 18 in. by 9 in., trace pattern piece 10, Sheet C (*dotted lines*) on to fresh paper and cut out. Place this pattern on blue material (wrong

PLATE IX
BABY DOLL

side) and cut out, allowing turnings ; machine and turn to right side, put it on doll and gather ankles, wrists, and neck. Pattern piece 4 shows pattern of glove. Cut out four pieces like this in cream material, a piece 8 in. by 2 in. for collar, and the same size for front of bonnet. A strip 7 in. by $2\frac{1}{4}$ in. and a circle of 2 in. diameter in blue will be required for back of bonnet. The gloves are sewn on the wrong side and the tops hemmed ; they are then turned right side out, put on to hands, and tied at the wrists with bows of orange ribbon.

The collar has the edges turned and slipstitched, and is put around neck with two orange beads acting as sham buttons. (Fig. 32c.) The blue 7 in. by $2\frac{1}{4}$ in. piece has its short edges hemmed, one long edge gathered into circular back of bonnet. The cream strip then has its edges turned and slipstitched, and is joined on to front of bonnet. The bonnet should be firmly sewn on to doll, and some extra stuffing may be added at back of head between doll's head and bonnet.

CHAPTER V

REAL DOLLS

I once had a sweet little doll dears,
The prettiest doll in the world,
Her cheeks were so red and so white dears,
And her hair was so charmingly curled.
—CHARLES KINGSLEY.

AMONG modern toys, stuffed dolls made of various fabrics hold a very popular place. Although requiring more skill than the toys already described, they really are not difficult to make. Four dolls are described in this chapter, all made on the same principle, the differences in each being only in the proportions of patterns, management of details and finishing, such as hair, faces, and extremities, and it is in these details that so much scope is afforded to the toy maker who possesses original ideas.

ARRABELLA. (Plate X.)

Materials—
  ½ yd. of flesh-coloured cotton material.
  Some sheep's wool.
  1d. skein of black embroidery cotton.
  Small length of red stranded cotton.
  ½ yd. of patterned artificial silk.
  2 yd. of black ribbon ½ in. wide.
  ½ yd. of black velvet ribbon 3 in. wide, or a piece of black velveteen.
  ½ yd. of white muslin with yellow spots.
  Some yellow Star silko.   Kapok to stuff.
  Cost about 3s.

Fig 30 A.

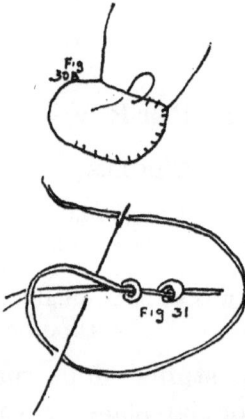

Fig 30 B.

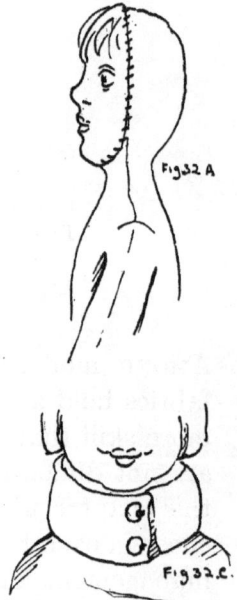

Fig 32 A

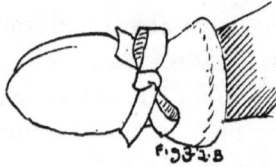

Fig 31

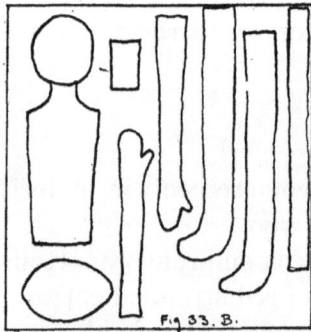

Fig 32 B

Fig 32 C.

Fig 33 A

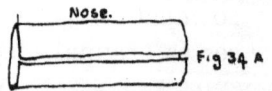

Nose.

Fig 34 A

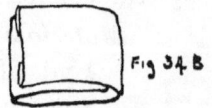

Fig 34 B

Fig 34 C

Fig 33. B.

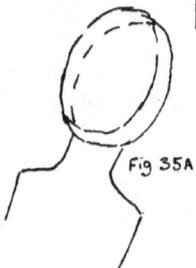

Fig 35A

Fig 35 B.

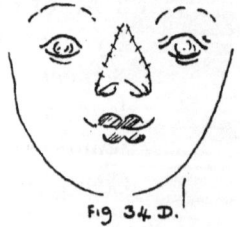

Fig 34 D.

It is important that the materials should be just right for the dressing of "Arrabella," or all her character and daintiness will be lost. The artificial silk for tunic and trousers should have a small yellow and red spotted pattern on a black ground ; Fig. 33A indicates the type of thing. "Arrabella " can, of course, be dressed in another colour scheme, but everything must be carefully thought out to go with it, and it is always best to choose a small pattern for the costume in keeping with the size of the dolls.

To make "Arrabella," cut out pattern pieces 1, 2, 3, 4, 5, 6, Sheet D. Fold $\frac{1}{2}$ yd. of flesh-coloured material in half so that it makes a double 18 in. square. Lay on pattern as in Fig. 33B, and cut out, allowing turnings. Each arm and leg and the body will have two pieces. The line marked with crosses at the base of head on pattern piece 1 shows where the front part of head should be cut away, the head and neck being in one piece only on the back.

Machine these pieces on wrong side and turn to right, leaving openings for stuffing between crosses. Using carbon paper, trace features on to face piece from pattern piece 4. Work them with black stem and backstitch all but the lips, which should be in red satin stitch. Lines on pattern piece 4 indicate direction of stitches. Now take nose piece and fold so that the two long edges meet in the centre (Fig. 34A), and then into three (Fig. 34B). The material should now form a rectangle of six thicknesses. Turn the top lower pieces over (Fig. 34C), form into nose shape and hem neatly on to face. (Fig. 34D.) Now put pattern piece 5 into back of head and front of neck, so that letters A, B, C, match, then oversew in face piece, slightly easing parts if necessary. Fig. 35A shows straight piece sewn on to back of head, and front of neck ready to receive face piece. Fig. 35B shows face piece sewn in. Now stuff; it is very important that the stuffing shall be firm in these more difficult toys, and that there shall be no weakness between neck and head, and between hands and arms. (Stuff body from bottom and head from side.) Turn in tops of arms and legs and oversew on to body. In this sewing see that it is strong, but see also that the arms and legs swing or flop forward and back easily, as this is half the charm of these soft dolls. Fig. 36 shows arm and leg sewn on; dotted lines show position of seams of leg and arm.

Hair. After sheep's wool has been prepared as described in the general instructions, sew a layer all around back of head with yellow cotton. (Fig. 37A.) Then sew two thick curly pieces of the wool to each side of the middle of head to form partings. Fig. 37B shows top of head with first piece of hair turned back and sewn. Fig. 37C shows that piece of hair turned over in place ready for the other side to be sewn on.

Dressing "Arrabella" (Fig. 38) shows patterns of garments. The squares represent inches, so first copy these patterns full size on paper. This is quite easy if sectional drafting paper is used. If this cannot be obtained, square up a piece of ordinary wrapping paper into inch squares with a ruler or tape measure, and draw pattern by counting the squares. Having made the patterns, lay that of trousers and tunic on the wrong side of artificial silk and cut out, allowing for turnings. Stitch all seams on wrong side except those parts marked *AB* and *CD* on trousers, and *EF* and *GH* on tunic, and *IJ* and *KL* on sleeve. Bind bottom of tunic, trouser

PLATE X
ARRABELLA

legs, and sleeves with black ribbon. Put trousers on
doll and sew them to waist with three pleats each side
of front and back. (Fig. 38B.) The bottoms of legs
will be open; sew these tight to legs. Cut strips of
muslin 30 in. by 5 in. for neck frill, and 14 in. by 2 in.
for each hand frill. Join these and fold the 5 in. width
in half and pleat around neck. Do the same with the
hand frills, folding the 2 in. width in half so that
the frills are double. Put on tunic, sew shoulder on to
doll, and sew neck over bottom of pleats of frill. Tie a
piece of black ribbon around neck to hide the join.
Put on sleeves and sew into arm holes. Bottoms of
sleeves will be open, as were the legs of the trousers; sew
them so that they fit tight to arms, and make bottoms
of sleeves come neatly over tops of hand frill pleats.
Arrange velvet at waist as a plain band, joined at side.

SHOES. The pattern is shown. (Fig. 38A.) Turn in
the top *M* and *N*, and sew right on to foot, making
seam in front. (Fig. 39A.)

Fig. 39B shows bottom of foot ribbon hemmed on to
form sole and cover join. Put a tassel made of yellow
star silko on to toes of shoes.

TOM THE NIGGER DOLL. (Plate XIA.)

Materials—

½ yd. of brown casement cloth.
Some black cable rug wool.
¼ yd. of red and white checked print.
⅛ yd. of blue linen.
Seven tiny white pearl buttons.
Two black boot buttons.
Black, red, and white embroidery cotton.
Kapok to stuff.
Cost about 1s. 6d.

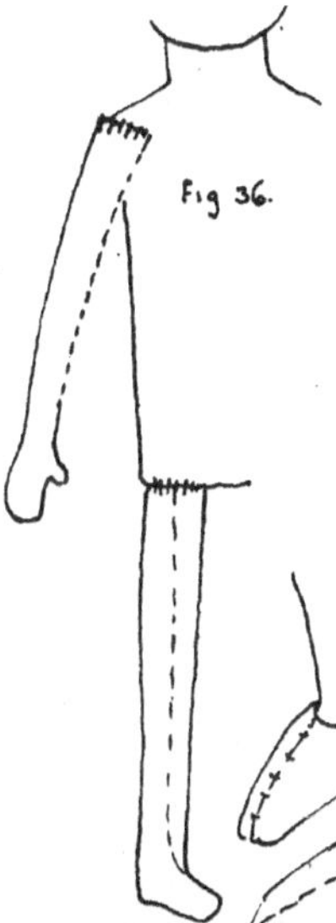

Fig 36.

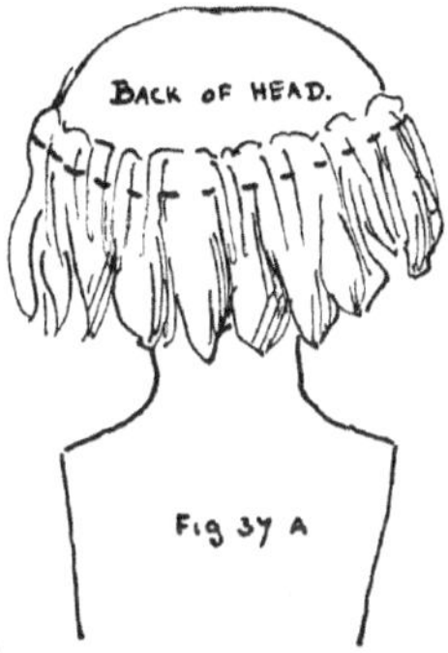

BACK OF HEAD.

Fig 37 A

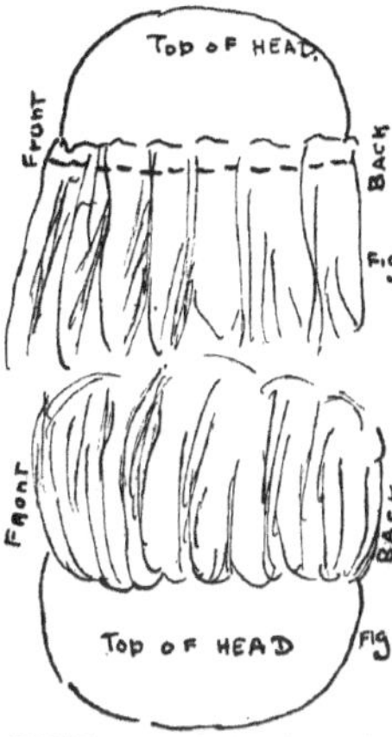

TOP OF HEAD.

Front

BACK

Fig 37 B

Front

BACK.

TOP OF HEAD

Fig 37 C

Fig 39 A.

Fig 39 B

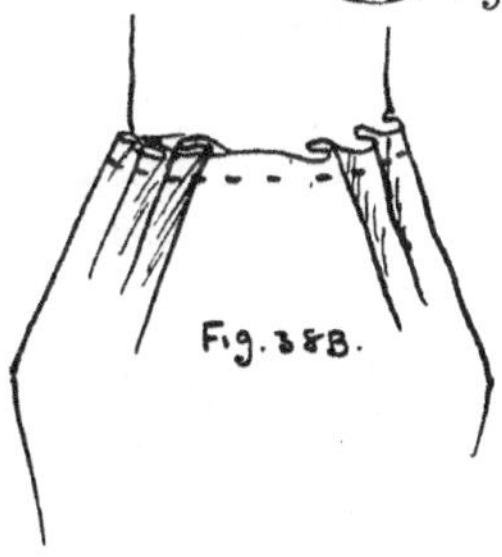

Fig. 38 B.

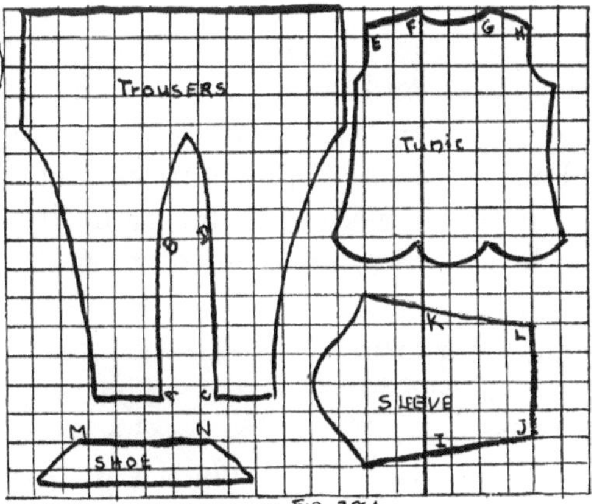

TROUSERS

TUNIC

E F G H

SLEEVE

K L

I J

SHOE

M N

Fig 38 A

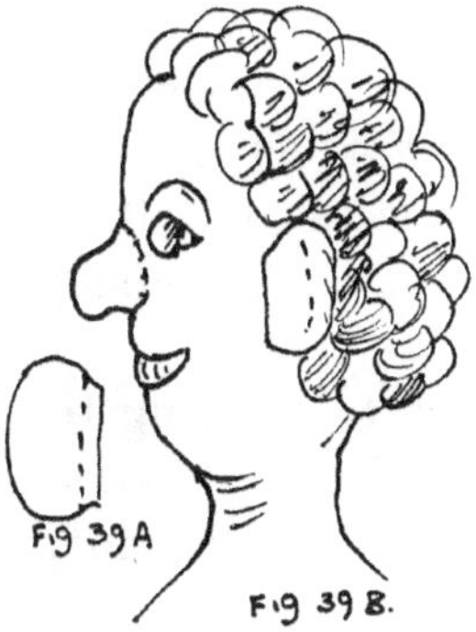

Fig 39 A

Fig 39 B.

TROUSERS

SHIRT

COLLAR

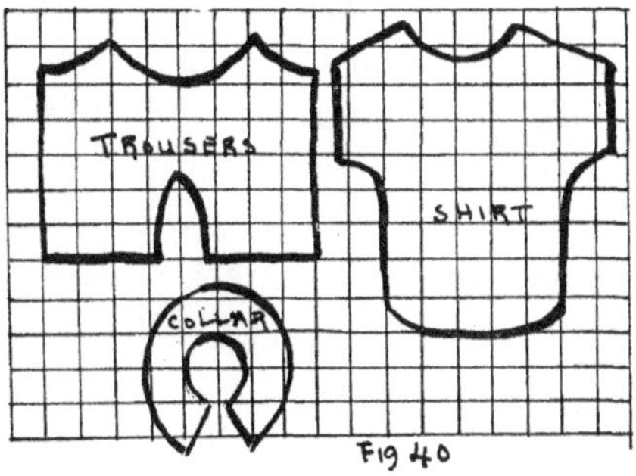

Fig 40

Cut out pattern pieces 7, 8, 9, 10, 11, 12, 13, and 14. Lay down on double brown casement cloth and mark outline on wrong side. Cut out. Each piece should be double and the ear, arms, and legs four times thick. Trace features on face piece, and stitch nose and turn right side out; stuff and hem on at *GH*, pattern piece 7. Work whites of eyes with white embroidery cotton, solid satin stitch. Put in boot buttons for pupils of eyes, pushing shanks right through material and sewing firmly. Work both eyelids and brows in black outline stitch. Work lips in red chain stitch, and put in teeth with black and white stitches as pattern piece 7.

Tack pieces together, fitting in head gusset so that letters *I* and *J* pattern pieces 7 and 12 match. Cut away front part of foot at line marked with crosses. Pattern piece 8. Put in front part of foot so that letters *ABCD* on piece 8 match same letters on piece 9. Fit sole piece into bottom of foot. The foot part is best sewn by hand. Machine rest of doll, turn right side out, and stuff. Sew on arms and legs as described in "Arrabella." (Fig. 36.) The seams of the legs in "Nigger Doll" will be at the sides. Stuff ears a little, and sew on. (Fig. 39B.) Fig. 39A shows ear turned back and stitched. Pick abroad rug wool and sew on in rows all over head. Stitch fingers as dotted lines, pattern piece 13. Take stitches right through hand and pull tight. Stitch toes in the same way as pattern piece 9. Gather around wrists and ankles and draw tight; this will give that delightful fat, podgy effect which is characteristic of this toy.

Dressing Doll (Fig. 40) shows pattern of clothing to the scale of one square to the inch. Make full-size patterns in paper. Cut out shirt in red checked print,

PLATE XIa
TOM THE NIGGER DOLL

PLATE XIb
JOSEPHINE WITH PLAITS

and trousers in blue linen. To cut trousers from $\frac{1}{8}$ yd. of linen it will be necessary to cut each leg separately and have seams at dotted lines. Cut collar of shirt in double material. Stitch seams of shirt and collar on wrong side, and turn to right side. Hem bottom of sleeves and shirt. Make an opening with a pleat in front of shirt; put on collar. Put shirt on doll and sew three pearl buttons down front of shirt. Now make trousers, stitch seams on wrong side; turn to right side; hem bottoms of legs and tops of trousers. Put on doll over shirt. Sew one pleat at each side from front to back to bring trousers in at the waist. Sew in pearl buttons to attach points on trousers to shirt.

JOSEPHINE WITH THE PLAITS. (Plate XIB.)

Materials—

$\frac{1}{2}$ yd. of flesh-coloured cotton material.

Some sheep's wool.

A piece of white stockinette or part of a worn vest.

$\frac{1}{2}$ yd. of red ribbon $\frac{1}{2}$ in. wide.

Ten small scarlet wooden beads.

Two small black wooden beads.

Small piece of red felt, small piece of brown felt.

A little red wool.

$\frac{1}{4}$ yd. of patterned print (white with blue and yellow spots).

$\frac{1}{2}$ yd. of round elastic (fine).

Water-colour paints.

Kapok to stuff.

Cost about 2s. 6d.

Cut out pattern pieces 13, 14, 15, 16, 17, and 18 from Sheet D. The making of "Josephine" is exactly the same as for "Nigger Doll Tom," except for the construction of the foot, the joining on of the head, and the fact that the face is painted instead of being worked.

PLATE XIc
A FRIENDLY GROUP

"Josephine's" neck and head are entirely separate from her body; heads put on in this way spring out at the back and can be made to form a chin in front in a most realistic way. Complete the making of the doll

as described before, all but the head and the feet. It
will be noticed that there is a sole for the foot; stitch
the leg and turn out, then put in the sole, making letters
match, and oversew on right side. The body is simply
an oblong bag. Make it and stuff it; then, form neck
into a circle and hem on as Fig. 41A. Paint features,
making "Josephine" a really pretty doll with pink
cheeks, red lips, and blue eyes. Stitch head seams.
Gather lower part of head and hem on to top of neck.
(Fig. 41B.) Stuff head and neck and sew up. The hair
is put on as described for "Arrabella" (Figs. 37A and
37B), but this time the sheep's wool is put on as long as
it can be obtained and in its natural colour, which gives
a beautiful ash blond effect.

After it has been sewn on the hair is carefully combed
and arranged in two long plaits, each tied with a large
bow of red ribbon.

Dressing "Josephine." She has a vest, knickers,
shoes, socks, and a dress. Fig. 42A shows pattern of
dress, knickers, and shoes; the skirt of dress is a straight
piece (36 in. by 7½ in.) Dotted lines on pattern pieces
13 and 17, Sheet D, show pattern of sock and vest
Cut these out from the unworn parts of an old vest; join
up on wrong side, and turn to right; hem bottom of vest
and put on to doll; couch a line of red wool along tops
of socks. Cut out soles of shoes in brown felt and uppers
in red; oversew uppers on to soles on right side; cut a
strip of red felt (5 in. by ¼ in.) for each shoe; attach this
to the back of shoes for straps around ankles (Fig. 42B);
put on doll and sew in a black bead to form button.

Machine seams of dress and bottom hem; turn ¼ in.
turning on bottom of bodice and pleat skirt under it
in ½ in. pleats; bring pointed bodice of dress over tops of

Fig 41A

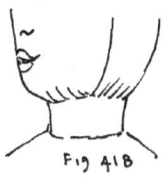
Fig 41B

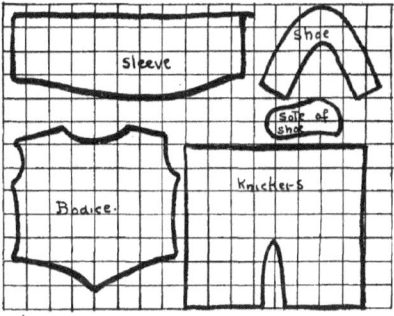
Sleeve

Shoe

Sole of shoe

Bodice

Knickers

Fig 42A

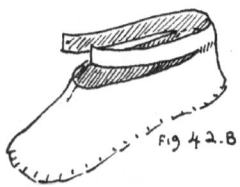
Fig 42.B.

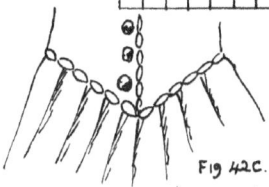
Fig 42C.

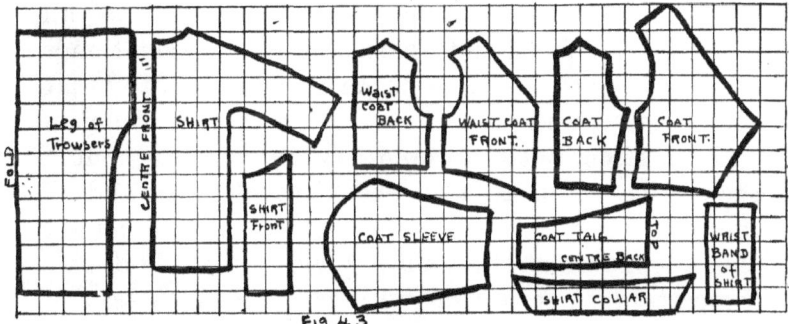
FOLD

Leg of Trowsers

CENTRE FRONT

SHIRT

WAIST COAT BACK

WAIST COAT FRONT.

COAT BACK

COAT FRONT.

SHIRT FRONT

COAT SLEEVE

COAT TAIL

CENTRE BACK

TOP

SHIRT COLLAR

WAIST BAND of SHIRT

Fig 43

Fig 44C

44A.

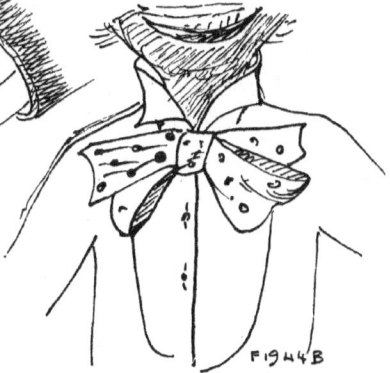
Fig 44B

pleats (Fig. 42c). Put in sleeves. These are puff sleeves gathered at armhole and tight to arm at bottom. Couch a line of red wool at bottom of sleeve and bodice down front of bodice. (Fig. 42c.) Sew in ten red beads to look like buttons. The dress should be slit down the back to get it on and sewn up when it is on the doll; a line of red wool should be couched at neck.

GOLLIWOG. (Plate XII.) The poor golliwog is surely one of the most loved and most badly treated of toys. By "badly treated" I mean that horrid representations of him can be bought at the stores for about sixpence each—nasty things which have lost all character and form, and whose only recommendation is that they are cheap. A golliwog seems to be a toy that should be big and noble, and, but for considerations of space, a larger pattern would have been given. But if the size of the pattern on Sheet D is doubled and all the instructions as to costume and detail are carried out, a truly wonderful golliwog will result. To double the pattern lay it on squared paper (1 in. squares) and mark around, then square up another piece of paper with 2 in. squares. Copy by proportion each piece of the pattern from the 1 in. squared paper on to the 2 in.

Materials for Golliwog—
　½ yd. of black sateen.
　Two linen buttons ¾ in. in diameter.
　Two black boot buttons.
　Small piece of black suede.
　¼ yd. of black patterned satin, either checked or striped.
　Small piece of gaily patterned silk for waistcoat.

A gentleman's worn-out shirt collar nicely
laundered.

¼ yd. of white cotton material.

¼ yd. of black velveteen.

¼ yd. of white silk.

¾ yd. of 1 in. wide gaily patterned ribbon.

Two brightly coloured fancy buttons.

Six brightly coloured fancy buttons of a different
pattern.

Piece of black fur for hair.

Wood wool for stuffing and kapok.

Cut out pattern pieces 19, 20, 21, 22, and 23, Sheet D.
All the points in the making of the golliwog have been
described in the three dolls which have been dealt with
before, the only difference being in the use of wood wool
for stuffing and fur for hair. Toys stuffed with wood
wool are harder and firmer, but greater care is required
in stuffing, the important thing being to put in a very
small piece at a time and to push it well in before the
next piece of stuffing is added. It is best to use kapok
for small parts, such as hands and noses, as wood wool
will not fill these successfully.

The fur for hair is simply cut to the shape of the head
and sewn firmly on.

Clothing (Fig. 43) shows patterns of the four garments. Shirt, trousers, waistcoat, and coat. Cut out
the shirt in white cotton material, and shirt front, collar,
and wrist band from a man's shirt collar. Do shoulder
and side seams of shirt, put on doll and sew shirt front in
place. Make it overlap slightly, as a shirt front would.
Sew on shirt, cuff at wrist (Fig. 44A), and collar at
neck, turning back points of collar and tying patterned

PLATE XII
GOLLIWOG

ribbon in large bow at neck. (Fig. 44B.) Cut out
trousers from patterned black satin ; make and sew on,
pleating on each side of waist, front, and back. Cut out
back of waistcoat from black sateen, and front from
brightly-patterned satin. Make and sew on, putting
fancy buttons to fasten. Cut out tail coat in black
velveteen and white silk for lining. The coat should be
made to take off and on. The easiest way to make the
coat is to tack lining to each piece, turn edge to edge,
and oversew each separate part back—two fronts, two
sleeves, and two tails. Then oversew coat together,
first sleeve seams, then underarm and shoulder seams ;
then put on tails. Put two fancy buttons above tails.
and white stitches to look like buttonholes on one
side of front and fancy buttons on the other. Make
shoes from suede, putting shiny side of suede outside.
Make them exactly as described for doll "Josephine,"
but without straps. Punch holes in front, and put in
shoe laces as in Fig. 44c.

CHAPTER VI

REAL ANIMALS

Ole Noah once he built the ark
And patched it up with hickory bark.
He went to work to load his stock;
He anchor'd the ark with a great big rock.
The animals went in three by three:
The bear, the flea, an' the humble bee.

THE successful making of animal soft toys depends
chiefly on the drawing of the silhouette of the particular
animal and the accuracy with which it is followed in
the sewing. As will soon be seen from the pattern
pieces, animals which stand on four legs are mainly
made up of four parts, a double silhouette of the whole
animal and a double silhouette of the legs and lower
part of the body. After some practice in making toys
with tested patterns the toy maker should be able to
design any animal which she wishes to make by simply
drawing the silhouette (slightly thickening the legs and
other thin parts). Animals with a distinctive silhouette,
such as camels, elephants, pigs, etc., make the most
successful toys. It will be found that if an animal such
as a sheep is attempted it is very likely to look, when
finished, like a strange sort of dog.

PORKER PIG. (Plate XIII.)

Materials—

¾ yd. of white Turkey towelling.
Length of black mending wool.
Piece of really stiff brown paper and some gloy.
Kapok to stuff.   Cost 9d.

Cut out pattern pieces 1, 2, 3, 4, 5, and 6, Sheet E.

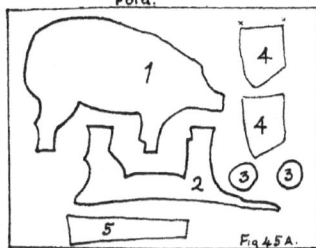

Fold.

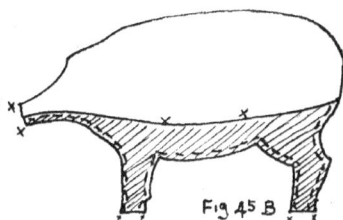

Fig 45 A.

Fig 45 B

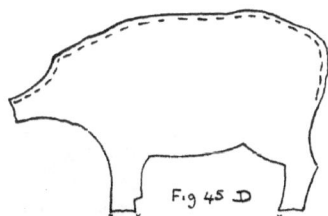

Fig 45 D

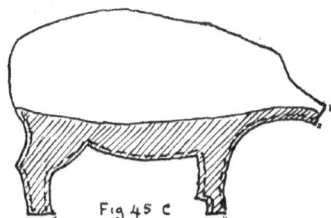

Fig 45 C

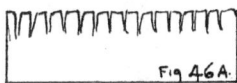

Fig 46 A.

Fig 46 B

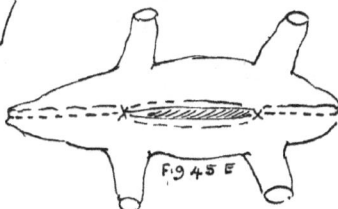

Fig 45 E

Fold.

Fig 50

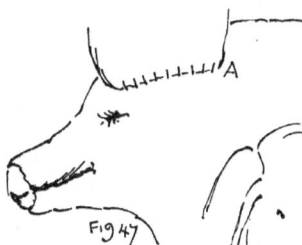

Fig 47

Fig 48

Fig. 49 B

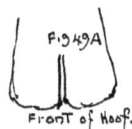

Fig 49 A

Front of Hoof.

Fold ¾ yd. of Turkey towelling in half so that it makes a double rectangle 18 in. by 13½ in. Lay down pattern pieces and paint outline, as Fig. 45A. Cut out, allowing wide turnings, as Turkey towelling frays easily. Tack pattern pieces 2 to pattern pieces 1, as Fig. 45B and 45C. Then place the parts Figs. 45B and 45C right side to

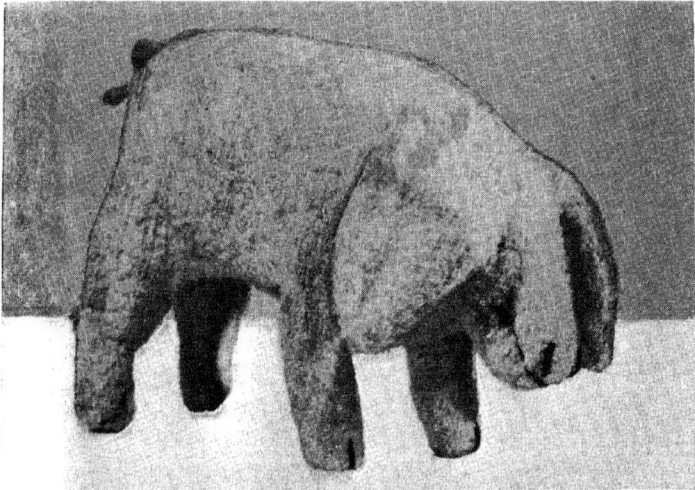

PLATE XIII
PORKER PIG

right side (the double leg pieces will then be touching each other), and tack above leg pieces. (Fig. 45D.) Machine or backstitch on tacking.

Machining is much the best for Turkey towelling toys, but if they have to be hand-sewn the stitching must be close. Leave open between crosses for snout and bottom of hoofs. Fig. 45E shows underneath part of pig, with seam running from snout to tail. The part between crosses is left open for stuffing. Now snip all corners as described. (Figs. 24A and 24B.) Turn right

side out and oversew round snout and bottoms of hoofs.
Stuff with Kapok, and when they are nearly stuffed
cut four pieces of brown paper 10 in. by 3 in., as Fig.
46A (snip top edge). Roll and stick with Gloy, and
push out fringed edge. (Fig. 46B.) Push these paper
supports into the tops of the legs, keeping the fringed
part upwards, stuff around them and finish stuffing
animal. Sew up opening and sew little pleats under
legs to keep them close to body. Stitch the ears on
wrong side, leaving opening between crosses for turning
out. Oversew openings on right side, then oversew
ears in position. (Fig. 47A.) Put in eye and mouth in
black wool backstitch. If the needle is passed right
through the head and back and pulled tight several
times, both for the eye and nose, a slightly modelled
effect is obtained.

Make two wool rings in the nose and buttonhole them.
(Fig. 48CD.) Make a long stitch in double black wool in
front of each hoof. (Fig. 49A.) Cut a piece of towelling
as pattern piece 5, roll it lengthwise and oversew it.
Then sew it in position at point A, pattern piece 1.
Curl it up and stitch to keep curl in place. (Fig. 49B.)

Porker pig can also be very successfully made in
black felt with white appliqué spots, or in grey or
fawn felt or flannelette.

POLAR BEAR. (Plate XIV.)

    Materials—
      1 yd. of Turkey towelling.
      Length of black wool.
      Some galvanized iron wire.
      Some strips of rag.   Kapok to stuff.
      Cost 1s.

Cut out pieces 7, 8, 9, 10, 11, Sheet E. Fold 1 yd. of Turkey towelling so that it makes a double square of 18 in. Place pattern pieces as Fig. 50, paint outline and cut out. The making of the polar bear is exactly as described for the porker pig, except that a forehead gusset has to be inserted, which is simply a matter of

PLATE XIV
POLAR BEAR

tacking pattern piece 9 in position, so that A and B, piece 9, fit A and B, piece 7. Also being a larger animal, the legs are wired and the finishings are a little different. When the polar bear is ready to stuff, cut two lengths of wire 10 in. long, bend each as Fig. 51A. Cut strips of rag and bind them firmly, especially the ends, which can be quite knobs. Push these pairs of wires into the legs. Fig. 51B shows back of the bear, and Fig. 51C front of the bear, as if the animal were transparent with wires in position. Stuff around wires, finish stuffing bear and sew up. Wired animals do not need the pleats under legs as the porker pig did, because the bending of the wire keeps legs in position.

The position of ears, eyes, and mouth are shown on pattern piece 7. The ears are sewn on upright, not turned back as porker pig's were. The paws have five vertical stitches, one in the centre of front and two on either side, about ⅜ in. apart.

The polar bear can also be very successfully made in short pile animal baize and stuffed with wood wool; it can then have proper small pink animal's eyes.

CAMEL. (Plate XV.)

Materials—
½ yd. of fawn-coloured felt.
Piece of royal blue felt.
Small piece of cerise felt.
Pair of medium brown and black animal's eyes.
Length of brown wool.
Length of galvanized wire.
Some rag.
Wood wool to stuff.
Cost 2s. 6d.

Cut out pattern pieces 12, 13, 14, 15, 16. Fold ½ yd. of felt into a double square of 18 in. Place pattern on material as Fig. 53A, paint outline and cut out. No turnings are needed on the felt. Fit camel together and tack exactly as described for porker pig, except that the sewing, instead of machining, must be done by hand and finely oversewn with matching Silko on the right side.

The wiring of the legs is exactly as for the polar bear,

except that the wires should be cut 14 in. long. The camel is stuffed with wood wool, which is a little more difficult to manage than Kapok. It is important that very small pieces are put in at a time and that each piece is well and firmly pushed down. The finishing of

PLATE XV
CAMEL

the camel is rather different to the other animals. For the eye, first cut two slits as shown in pattern piece 12, letter *F*. Take a piece of felt about ¾ in. square, put the eye into the centre of it (as described under general instructions). Fig. 53B shows the eye in position on patch, now put the patch behind the eye slit in head, so that the eye shows through and slit looks like an eyelid, backstitch an oval around eye to keep patch in

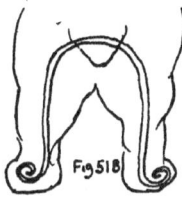

Fig 51 A

Fig 51 B

Fig 51 C

Fig 52.

53 B

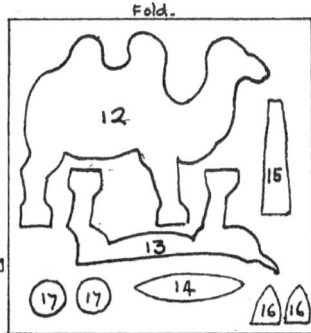

Fold.

12

15

13

17 17 14 16 16

Fig 53 A

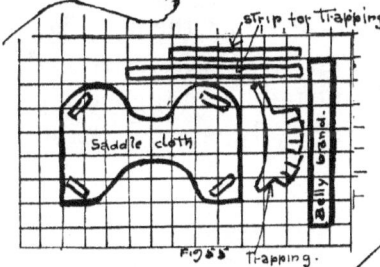

strip for Trapping

Saddle cloth

Belly band

Fig 55 Trapping.

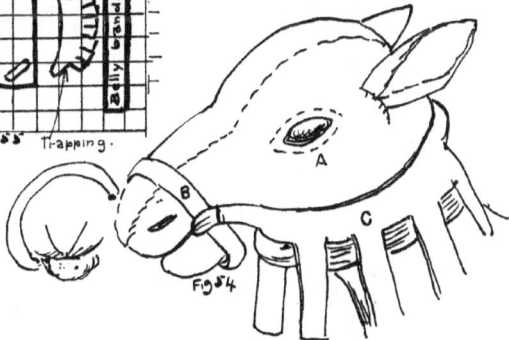

A

B

C

Fig 54

Fold

3

2

5 5

Fig 56 A

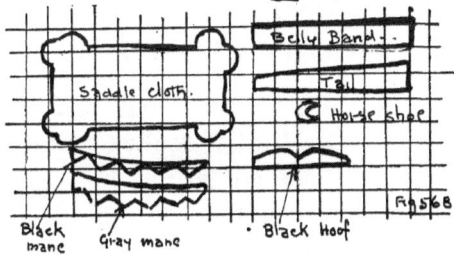

Belly Band.

Saddle cloth.

Tail

Horse shoe

Black mane   Gray mane   Black Hoof

Black Hoof

Fig 56 B

position. Fig. 54A shows eye in position and line of backstitch. To put in the ears, a slit is cut in the head *DE*, pattern piece 12, and ears are slipped in place and sewn. The camel wears a saddle cloth and belly band and some trappings on its head. Fig. 55 shows patterns of these to the scale of one square to 1 in. Make full-size patterns (as described for doll "Arabella"). Cut out saddle cloth in blue felt, belly band, and strip for decoration in cerise felt, backstitch on small pieces of cerise felt as decoration on corners of saddle cloth, *GH*, pattern piece 12, sew belly band in position and saddle cloth over it, as shown in pattern piece 12. Cut a strip of blue felt and sew around the nose of camel. (Fig. 54B.) Cut two shaped fringed trappings in blue and weave a strip of cerise in and out them. (Fig. 54C.) Sew them in position as Fig. 54. Mark nostril and nose of camel in brown wool, roll and hem tail, and put in at *C*, pattern piece 12. Mark four brown wool stitches on each hoof.

DONKEY. (Plate XVI.)

Materials—

    ¾ yd. of grey felt.
    Small piece of black felt.
    Small piece of yellow felt.
    Small piece of orange felt.
    Length of galvanized wire.
    Pair of large brown and black animal's eyes.
    Wood wool to stuff.   Cost 2s.

Cut out pattern pieces 1, 2, 3, 4, 5, Sheet F. Fold grey felt so that it makes a double rectangle 18 in. by 13½ in. Place pattern as Fig. 56A. Cut out bottoms of hoofs (pattern piece 4) in black felt. Tack parts of donkey together as described for pig and camel. Leave an opening between crosses for stuffing at piece 2, and on the head piece 1 for putting in eyes and details

PLATE XVI
DONKEY

of head. The finishing and details of donkey are differ-ent from other animals and need directions. Fig. 56B shows patterns of saddle cloth, belly band, grey and black mane, hoof, horseshoe, and tail. Draw them full size. Cut out four hoofs in black felt and four horse-shoes in grey felt. Hem black hoofs in position, as

Figs. 57A and 57B. Hem grey horseshoes on bottom of hoofs as Fig. 57C. Cut out tail in grey felt, roll it and hem, cut ends in a fringe for about 2 in. The position of tail is shown at C pattern piece 1, and Fig. 57D shows how it should look when sewn on. Cut out the mane, one piece in grey felt and two in black. Tack the three pieces together, the black pieces on either side of the grey. Place mane in position between letters EF on body pieces. (The forehead piece will have to be cut from B to E.) Sew firmly. Fig. 58A shows mane in position. Put in ears and eyes as before described. Hem on black nostril and mouth as shown in pattern piece 1. The donkey wears a halter, which is just a band of orange felt threaded in a bodkin and passed right through the mouth and sewn to another band of orange felt which passes around the nose; a small square of yellow felt covers the join. (Fig. 58B.)

Cut out belly band in yellow felt and saddle cloth in orange, fasten belly band to donkey, and then fasten saddle cloth over it.

Dog Toby. (Plate XVII.)

> *Materials—*
> ¼ yd. of white long pile animal baize 50 in. wide.
> ⅜ yd. will make two dogs.
> Pair of medium-size brown and black dog's eyes.
> Small piece of red felt.
> Some black embroidery cotton.
> Length of wire.
> Wood wool to stuff.   Cost 1s. 8d.

Cut out pattern pieces 6, 7, 8, 9, 10, 11. Toys in thick animal baize must have each part of pattern cut separately; so it is no use folding material as has been

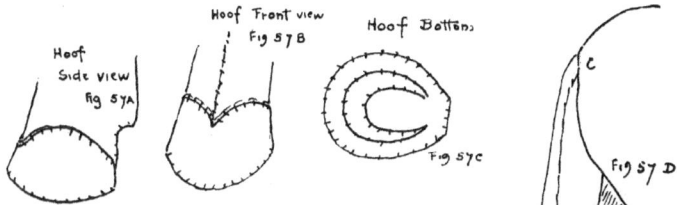

Hoof
Side View
Fig 57A

Hoof Front view
Fig 57 B

Hoof Bottom

Fig 57C

c

Fig 57 D

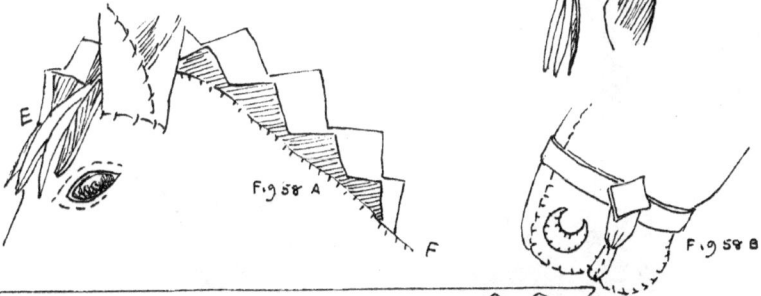

E

Fig 58 A

F

Fig 58 B

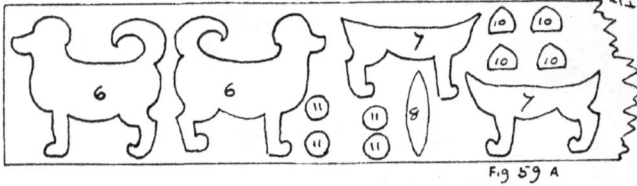

6 6 7 10 10 10 10 11 11 8 11 11 7

Fig 59 A

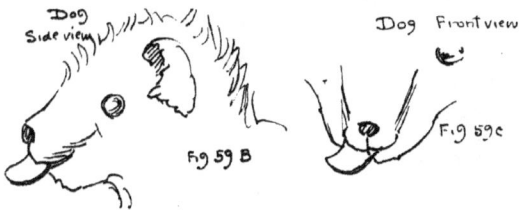

Dog
Side view

Dog Front view

Fig 59C

Fig 59 B

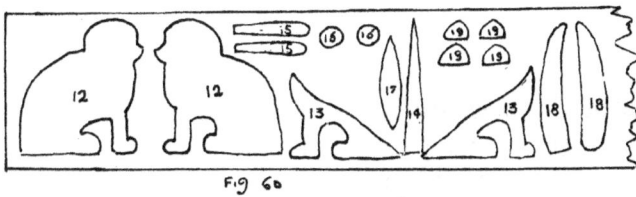

12 12 13 15 15 16 16 17 14 19 19 19 19 13 18 18

Fig 60

done for other toys. Place material wrong side up and
lay out pattern as Fig. 59A. It will be noticed that the

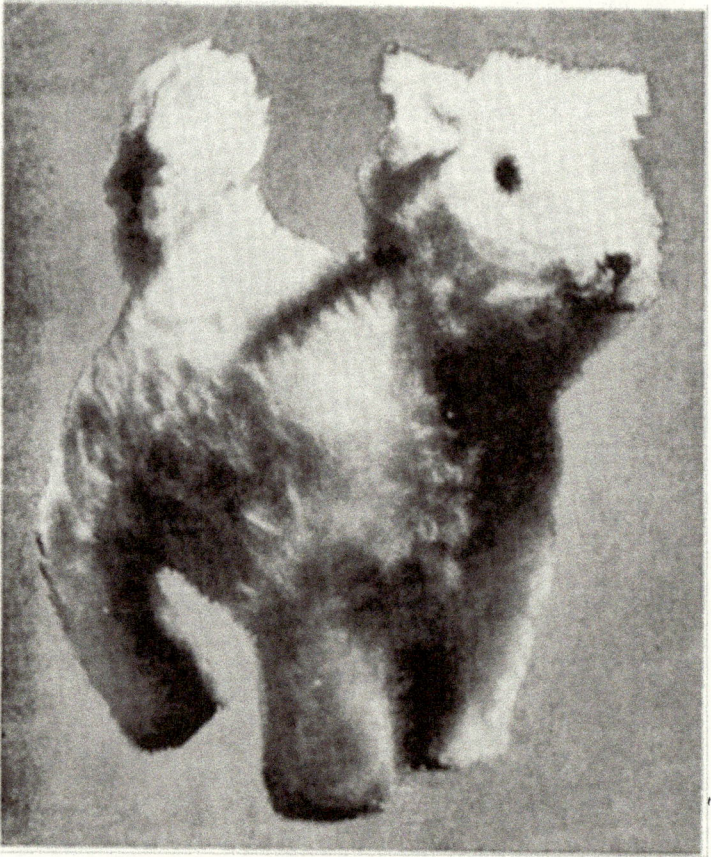

PLATE XVII
DOG TOBY

two sides of the dog are turned so that the material
which has a right and wrong side will face correctly,
also that all the pattern pieces are placed upright, so

that the pile of the baize will lie in the same direction. There is very little difference in the making of this and the other animals described. Fit parts together, making letters on pattern pieces; match, tack, and machine or hand stitch on wrong side and turn to right. The chief difficulty will be found in the management of the long pile of baize. The ears are best made by turning edge to edge and oversewing on right side. The eyes are put in as described in general instructions. The nose and mouth are worked in black backstitch, the black tip of nose in satin stitch. A red felt tongue is cut out as pattern piece 9 and sewn in position. Fig. 59B and 59C show ear, eye, nose, and tongue in position.

BLACK CAT. (Plate XVIII.) This is a sitting-down animal. They are, on the whole, easier to make than standing ones, the principle of designing them being very much the same. A good silhouette of the side view (sitting down) and then the front legs and underneath part of body double.

Materials—

    ¼ yd. of black animal plush 50 in. wide will make two cats.

    Some horsehair.

    Pair of small yellow eyes.

    Length of orange ribbon (narrow).

    Kapok to stuff.

Cut out pattern pieces 12, 13, 14, 15, 16, 17, 18, 19. Cut ¼ yd. of plush into two rectangles 25 in. by 9 in.; use one of these single. Fig. 60 shows pattern pieces laid out on wrong side of material. Mark outline and cut out, allowing wide turnings. Fig. 61A shows pattern pieces 11 and 12 placed right side to right side and tacked. Fig. 61B shows the same pieces for the other side of cat. Fig. 61c shows the same pieces placed in position with back gusset and forehead between them.

PLATE XVIII
BLACK CAT

The seams marked with crosses. Figs. 61A and 61B are then put together and stitched, leaving an opening between *O–O* for stuffing. The underpart of paws are then oversewn in position from the right side, making letters of pattern pieces match. The cat stuffed and sewn up.

Make and stuff tail, put on at *A*, pattern piece 13. Put on ears and eyes as described for other animals and shown in Fig. 62B.

Put in horsehair whiskers by threading horsehair in needle and sewing in position, and cutting required length after they are sewn. Tie orange ribbon around neck, making a bow at back.

If a larger sitting down animal is made, the front legs would need to be wired just as the standing animals were. In this small cat it will only be necessary to sew pleats to keep the legs close to the underneath part of the body.

CHAPTER VII

MASCOTS AND FREAK TOYS

I went to the animal's Fair ;
All the Birds and the Beasts were there.
By the light of the Moon the Giddy Baboon
Was combing his auburn hair.
The Monkey fell out of his bunk,
And slid down the Elephant's trunk ;
The Elephant sneezed and fell on his knees,
And what became of the Monkey—Monkey—Monk ?

SOME solemn people say that mascots are foolish things. Some say that all play and make-belief are only for children, and should be put away with other childish things. It is certain, however, that the brightly-coloured mascot dangling at the back window of a motor-car can give a distinct feeling of pleasure to many a car owner. Also that the gay freak doll or animal in My Lady's Boudoir adds just the needed spot of interest and colour. In modern life the form these mascots take is legion, and many of them are exceedingly clever in design. Some bear no resemblance to any figure, animal, or bird which ever lived, while others are very like some distinctive type and are simply made in patterned or odd materials. The first of these toys to be described is a puppet. The idea of the puppet show is "as old as the hills," and puppets have been made from earliest times in all parts of the world. The principal of the working of puppets is best known by the ever popular Punch and Judy show. The odd actions, fun, and amusement to be got out of these

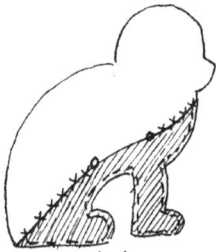

Fig 61 A

Fig 61 B.

Fig 61 C

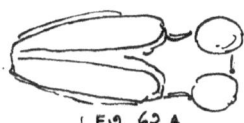

Fig. 62 A.

Fig 62 B.

Fig 63A

Puppet Show.
Front view

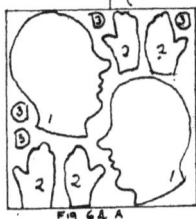

Fig 64 A

4"

Fig 64 B

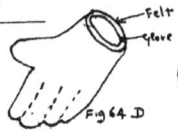

Felt
glove

Fig 64 D

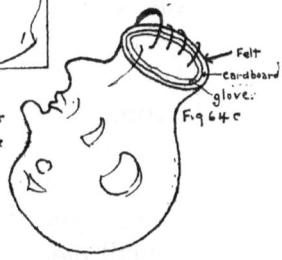

Felt
cardboard
glove.

Fig 64 C

Puppet Show
Side view

Fig 63 B

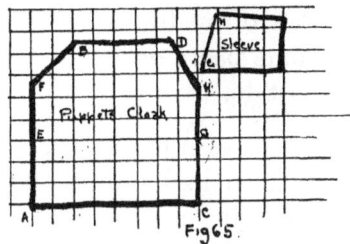

Sleeve

Puppets Cloak

Fig 65

puppets is amazing. Properly manipulated, they really become almost human.

The making of one puppet is described, but by changing the type of head, features, and costume almost any character can be represented. Wonderful results can be obtained in schools, clubs, Girl Guide companies, etc., by taking the puppet show idea, making puppets to represent the characters in a play and getting some of the clever pupils or members to work a puppet show for the entertainment of the rest. Quite an effective stage can be made by cutting an aperture in a large sheet of three-ply wood, fixing it behind a table covered with a large cloth. The table should be just far enough from a wall for the manipulator of the puppet to hide comfortably. (Figs. 63A and 63B.)

ARCHIBALD THE PUPPET. (Plate XIX.)

Materials—

A 9 in. square of white felt.

Piece of thin cardboard.

Tops of three of the largest fingers of a worn-out glove.

¼ yd. of brightly-patterned velveteen, black, red, and yellow.

Small piece of yellow sateen.

Pair of medium-size brown and black eyes.

Some paste or glue. Kapok to stuff.

Cost 1s.

Cut out pattern pieces 1, 2, and 3. Sheet G, Fig. 64A, shows pattern laid out on 9 in. square of white felt. Cut out, leaving NO turnings. The profile of face must be very accurately cut. Oversew finely on right side of head and hands. Cut a piece of cardboard 5 in. by

PLATE XIX
ARCHIBALD THE PUPPET

4 in., make it into a roll around the middle finger ; either sew or glue in place. (Fig. 64B.) Stuff the head firmly with Kapok and push the cardboard roll up into the

centre. Put a glove finger on to the second finger of the right hand, cover finger with glue, push it up inside the roll of cardboard. Withdraw finger of hand without pulling out glove finger. Sew bottom of glove finger to bottom of cardboard and felt neck of head; Fig. 64c shows this being done. Make ear, slightly stuff, and sew on. Stuff fingers of hands and make three lines of stitching to separate fingers (as pattern piece 2). Stuff hands, put glove fingers on fourth finger and thumb of right hand, cover them with glue, push them into hands, and remove finger and thumb without pulling glove fingers out of hands. Sew cut edges of glove fingers to felt. Fig. 65 shows pattern of puppet's cloak drawn to scale. Draw pattern full-size as described for doll's clothing ("Arrabella," Fig. 38A). Cut out in velveteen. Join up side seams *AB–CD*, leaving openings *EF* and *GH* for sleeves. Make sleeves and insert in cloak, making letters on pattern pieces match. Hem bottom of cloak and sleeves. Cut a band of yellow sateen 20 in. by 4 in., make it into a circular strip, and fold the 4 in. in half. (Fig. 66A.) Pleat around neck of puppet. (Fig. 66B.) Sew neck of cloak over bottom of pleats. Slightly gather bottom of sleeves and hem into tops of hands. The puppet is now ready to perform. Fig. 66c shows puppet as if it were transparent with the hand inside ready to manipulate it.

BROTHER RABBIT. (Plate XX.)

Materials—

$\frac{3}{4}$ yd. of white Turkey towelling 18 in. wide.

Five plain white linen buttons $\frac{1}{2}$ in. in diameter.

Two plain white linen buttons $\frac{3}{4}$ in. in diameter.

Some black wool. Some stiff paper.

PLATE XX
BROTHER RABBIT

Piece of scarlet cotton material (fugi or casement
cloth).
Kapok to stuff.   Cost 8d.

Cut out pattern pieces 4, 5, 6, 7, and 7A, Sheet G.
Fold Turkey towelling into a double rectangle 18 in. by
13½ in. Lay out pattern on double material as shown
in Fig. 67A. Paint outline and cut out, allowing large
turnings. Cut linings for ears in red. Machine on
wrong side, leaving openings between crosses for
stuffing. Turn to right side and stuff, sew up openings,
fold and sew on ears as Figs. 67B and 67C. Sew scarlet
patches on bottom of the paws (Fig. 67D), and back of
tail. Sew the legs on as shown (Plate XX), sew them
rather loosely, so that they will move forward and back.
Sew the tail in the centre of lower part of back. (Fig
67E.) Sew in buttons as shown in pattern piece 4, using
large ones for eyes, small one for nose, and four small
ones down the front. Paint nose and front buttons
red, and the eyes as shown in pattern piece 4. Work
eyebrows and nose in black wool.

Brother Rabbit is a really delightful mascot. The
above instructions show how it can be very cheaply
made, but if a larger and more expensive toy is desired
the size of pattern can be doubled, and long pile white
animal baize used, and red felt for the patches and
lining of ears.

PENTAGONAL BALL. (Plate XXI.) This can hardly
be called a freak or a mascot, but it is put in this section
because, besides being a delightful toy for a small child,
it is really a thing of beauty and would add a pleasing
touch of colour to any room.

Materials—

A 3½ in. square of felt in twelve different colours,
or a 4 in. square of left-over material in twelve
different colours.

Kapok to stuff.

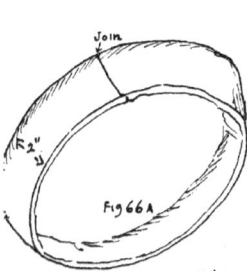

Join

Fig 66 A

Fig. 66B

Fig 66.c

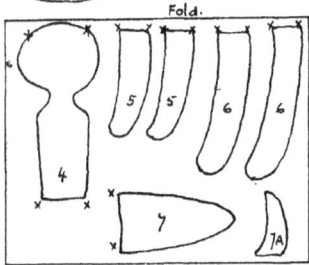

Fold.

5 5 6 6

4

7

7A

Fig. 67 A

Fig 67 B

Fig 67 C

Fig 67. D.

2

1

Fig 68 A

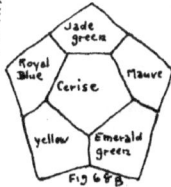

Jade green

Royal Blue Cerise Mauve

yellow Emerald green

Fig 68 B

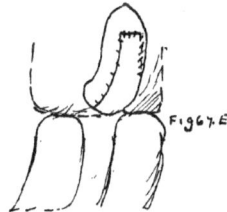

Fig 67. E

Fg 68 c.

Mauve

Cerise Fawn.

Green orange

Yellow Black

Grey

Paper

Fig 68 D

Fold

12 10 12

12 13

9

8 14

Fig 69.A

ear lining.

Yellow Felt

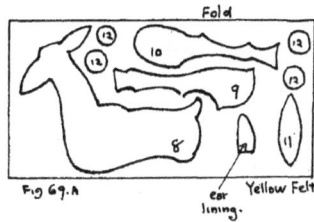

9 8 10

Head

Black Felt

Fig 69 B

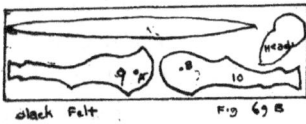

It is difficult to put a cost to this ball, it is a good way of using up left-over pieces of felt and other material. The ball is easiest made in felt for that shown in Plate XXI, the colours used are cerise, emerald green, lemon yellow, royal blue, jade green, mauve, black, scarlet, fawn, orange, grey, and purple. Cut out pattern piece 21, Sheet H, which is a regular

PLATE XXI
PENTAGONAL BALL

pentagon of $2\frac{1}{4}$ in. side, lay pattern on each of the twelve pieces of felt, mark outline very carefully with chalk, and cut out (no turnings). Now take the side of one pentagon and firmly oversew it to the side of another. Fig. 68A shows this done, and the pentagons numbered 1 and 2. Take another pentagon and over-sew it to pentagon No. 2 on the side marked with crosses ; continue adding pentagons until there are five, forming a sort of ring or conical shape. Then oversew another pentagon into the centre of the shape. This last pentagon would be the cerise one. (Fig. 68B.) This is half the ball. Join the other six pentagons into a like shape, then put then together (Fig. 68c), oversew all parts except two sides of pentagons, which must be left open for stuffing. Turn to the right side, stuff firmly, and sew up opening. The ball can be quite successfully made of left-over pieces of silk and velvet. To do this cut out twelve pentagons in paper—ordinary note paper will do—or thin wrapping paper. Tack each piece of paper to a piece of silk or velvet, cut out material, allowing ¼ in. turnings. Turn silk over edge of paper and tack as Fig. 68d. Oversew pieces together on wrong side, turn out and stuff as described for felt ball.

WILLIAM GOAT. (Plate XXII.) This toy is made of felt in three colours and jointed.

Materials—
    ¼ yd. of lemon yellow felt.
    ⅛ yd. of black felt.
    Small piece of jade green felt.
    Pair of small yellow and black animal's eyes.
    Four sets of pins and washers for animal's joints.
    Wood wool to stuff.
    Cost 2s.

Cut out pattern pieces 8, 9, 10, 11, 12, 13, and 14, Sheet G. Fold ¼ yd. of yellow felt into a double rectangle 18 in. by 9 in., lay out pattern pieces 8, 9, 10, 11, 12. Make a tracing of ear pattern from pattern piece 8, as far as arrow marks for ear lining, Fig. 69 show these pieces laid out on yellow felt. Fold ⅛ yd. of black felt into a double rectangle 18 in. by 4½ in. Lay out pattern pieces 9, 10, 13, and trace black part of head pattern piece 8 and lay down. (Fig. 69b.) Mark outline carefully with chalk and cut out, NO turnings.

PLATE XXII
WILLIAM GOAT

There should be four yellow legs, four yellow under-
hoofs, four black legs, two upperbody pieces, one
yellow underbody piece, black forehead, yellow ear
lining, yellow head pieces for putting on in appliqué in
black. Cut out horn as pattern piece 14, and parts

marked in shaded lines on pattern pieces 9 and 10 in
jade green. Cut several ¼ in. strips of jade green.
Arrange these green strips on body, as shown in Plate
XXII, and pattern piece 8. Tack them in place and
hem on. Cut green and black patches for legs, hem on
these and black head pieces. Fit in forehead piece and
ear lining, make horn, stuff it, and sew in place. Put
in eye (Fig. 70A shows all this). Fig. 70B shows top of
head with ear linings put in. Note large opening for
eye cut in black felt, and yellow band left around eye.
Fit in black underbody, making letters CD, pattern
pieces 13 and 8, match. Oversew all parts of goat on
right side, leaving openings for stuffing and putting in
joints between crosses. Figs. 71A, 71B, and 71C shows
body fitted together, leg, and hoof.

The joints consist of a split wire pin (Fig. 72A), a
metal washer (Fig. 72B), and a wooden washer (Fig.
72C). Fig. 72D shows the pin and two washers fitted
together ready to go inside the animal. Make a small
hole at E and F, pattern piece 8 (both sides of body),
push the pins through so that the wooden washers rest
tight against inside of felt. The pins should poke out
through animal as shown in Fig. 71C. Now make holes
in black parts or insides of legs at points shown A and
B, pattern pieces 9 and 10. Push the pins through to
insides of legs, put on wood and metal washer, and
open pin, curl back very tightly on discs. Fig. 72E
shows two squares which are intended to represent the
two materials, yellow of body and black of leg. The
dotted line shows second disc as if material was transparent. The curled ends of pin are also shown.

The two discs must be very tightly brought together
or the joints of the animal will be wobbly. The goat

should have its four legs joined to body with these
metal pins. Stuff very firmly with wood wool and sew
up openings.

THE GAY BIRD. (Plate XXIII.)

Materials—

$\frac{1}{4}$ yd. of lemon yellow felt.
$\frac{1}{8}$ yd. of black felt.
Some galvanized iron wire.
Pair of small black and white eyes.
Piece of stiff cardboard.
Wood wool and Kapok to stuff.
Cost 1s. 8d.

Cut out pattern pieces 15, 16, 17, 18, 19, and 20,
Sheet G. Fold $\frac{1}{4}$ yd. of yellow felt into a double
rectangle 18 in. by 9 in., lay out pattern pieces 15, 17,
19, as Fig. 73A. Fold $\frac{1}{8}$ yd. of black felt into a double
rectangle 18 in. by $4\frac{1}{2}$ in., lay out pattern pieces 17 and
16 and black head piece traced from pattern piece 15.
Fig. 73B shows black felt with pattern laid out. Cut
out, allowing NO turnings. Cut out three double red
feathers and one double black as pattern piece 18, and
comb as Fig. 74A in red. Cut also some red and black
strips $\frac{3}{16}$ in. wide, and some red $\frac{1}{4}$ in. wide, also inside
of beak in red as pattern piece 20.

Lay pattern piece 15 again on material and trace
position of red and black bands. Hem or run these on,
also black head, oversew in place inside of beak,
making letters *GHI*, pattern pieces 15 and 20, match.
Put in eye, oversew edges of four feathers, stuff them
with Kapok, and sew up openings. Fit them in
between two pieces of body of bird, starting with the
black one at *EF*, pattern piece 15, and arranging the

others in a row (Fig. 74c). Fit in underpart of body, making letters *JK*, pattern pieces 15 and 16, match. Stuff with wood wool. For the foot there should be a

PLATE XXIII
THE GAY BIRD

black and yellow piece as pattern piece 17, and for the leg two yellow pieces as pattern piece 19. Cut cardboard as foot piece, and two lengths of wire 8 in. long for each leg, bend the end of wire into loops and sew

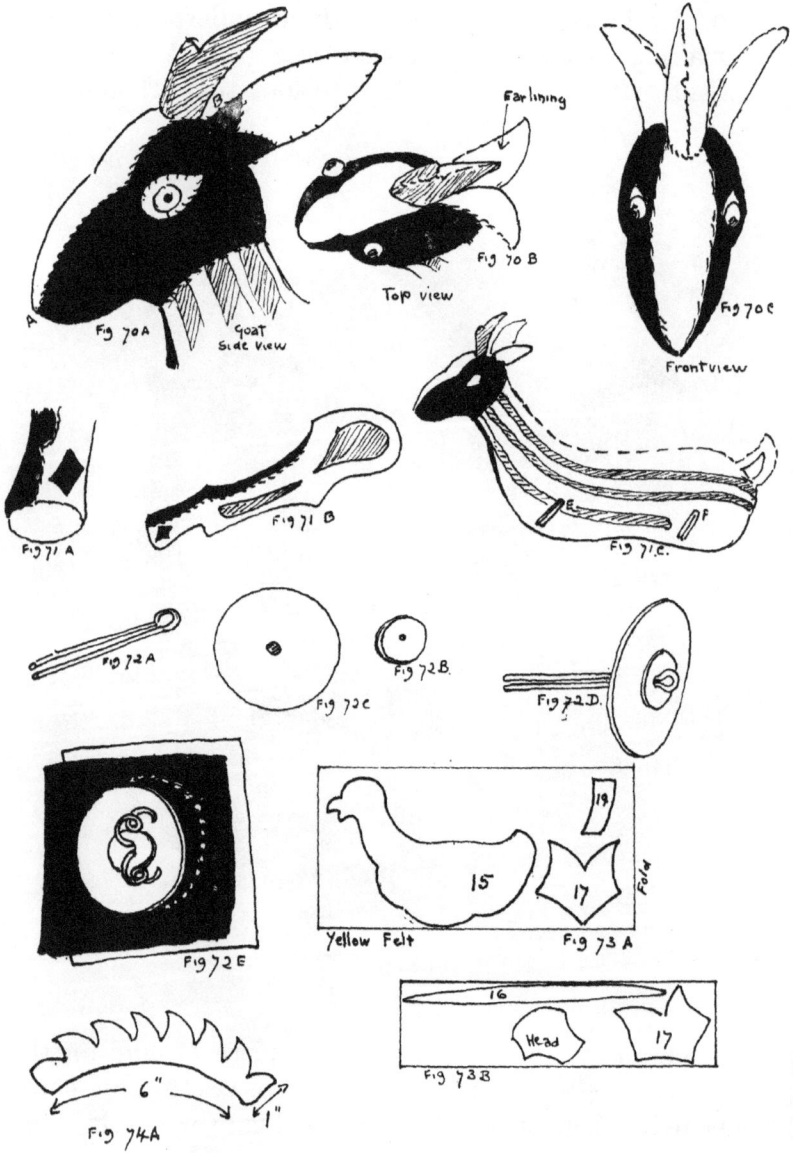

Ear lining

Fig 70 B

Top view

Fig 70 A

A
Goat
Side View

Front view

Fig 70 C

Fig 71 A

Fig 71 B

Fig 71 C

Fig 72 A

Fig 72 B.

Fig 72 C

Fig 72 D.

Fig 72 E

Yellow Felt

19

15

17

Fold

Fig 73 A

16

Head

17

Fig 73 B

6"

1"

Fig 74 A

two pieces firmly on to cardboard as Fig. 75. Oversew
black and yellow felt edge to edge to cover cardboard
foot. Oversew leg pieces, bend wire at a right angle to
foot cover with leg pieces, which should have their
lower part sewn firmly to foot piece at angle of wire.
Stuff legs with Kapok—wood wool is too hard. Push
wires well up into body of bird, and hem tops of legs
to body. The position of the legs on the bird is about
midway between head and tail and just at the front of
black underbody with yellow sides. There are two red
strips down the front of each leg extending on to the
top of the foot. Fig. 75B shows leg and foot with red
strip indicated with shaded lines.

SPOTTY ELEPHANT. (Plate XXIV.)

Materials—

½ yd. of spotted print 36 in., red, black, and white.
Piece of black casement cloth.
Small piece of black felt.
Small piece of white felt.
Piece of galvanized wire.
Two small black beads.
Kapok to stuff.   Cost 8d.

Cut out pattern pieces 22, 23, 24, 25, and 26. Fold
½ yd. of print into a double square of 18 in., lay out
pattern as Fig. 76. Mark outline and cut out, allowing
¼ in. turnings. Cut out linings of ears and under-parts
of hoofs in black casement cloth. Tusks in white felt
as pattern piece 26, and tail in black felt, a strip 5 in.
long and 1¼ in. wide, tapering to ½ in.

The making of the elephant is exactly as described for
other animals—pig, polar bear, etc. (the legs should be
wired). The only difference being in the ear, tusk, tail,

and eye. The position of ear is marked *AB* on pattern piece 22. The ear is made and put on as described for pig (Figs. 47 and 48), except that the back part of the

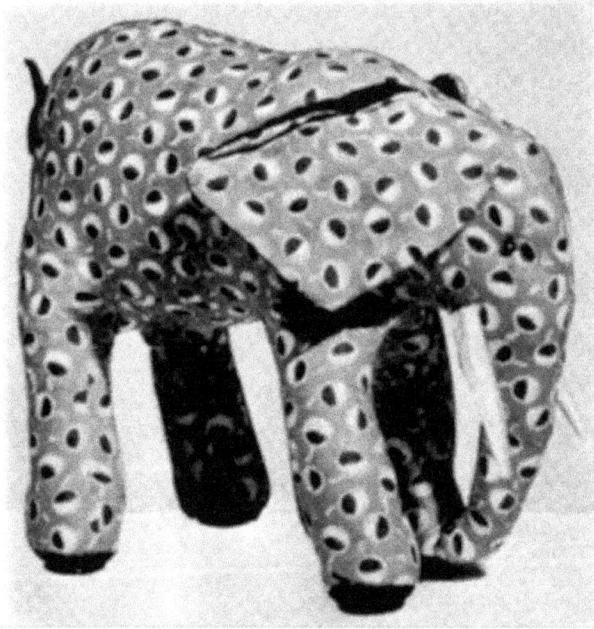

PLATE XXIV
SPOTTY ELEPHANT

ear is folded out to show the black lining. (Fig. 76B.) For the tusk the piece of white felt is rolled and hemmed and inserted at *CD*, pattern piece 22. The tail piece is rolled and hemmed as the tusk, but a piece of wire is inserted in the centre. This is shown where the tail is drawn as if it were transparent. (Fig. 76C.) The black beads are sewn in for eyes, and needle passed forward and back through head to cause a slightly modelled effect.

Fig 74 B

Fig 74 C

Fold.

22

25

23

Fig 76 A

Fig 75 A

Fig 75 B

Fig 76 B.

Fig 76 C.

Fig 77 A

31

29

27

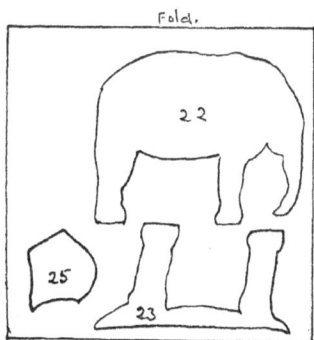

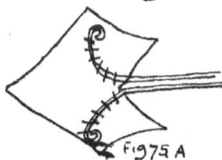

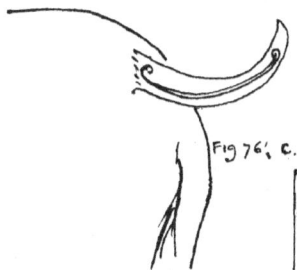

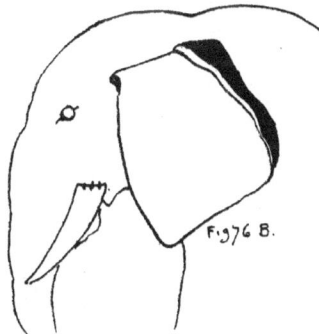

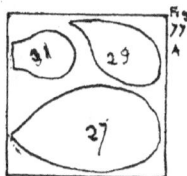

Jade green
Felt

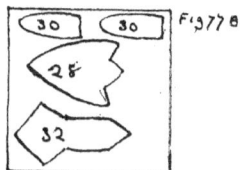

Fig 77 B

30

30

28

32

orange Felt.

STICK BIRD. (Plate XXV.)

Materials—

$\frac{1}{8}$ yd. of patterned print 36 in., orange, jade green, and white.

Two 7 in. squares of jade green felt.

Two 7 in. squares of orange felt.

A bamboo or other stick $\frac{5}{8}$ in. in diameter.

A pair of small bird's eyes.

Some stiff cardboard.

Kapox to stuff.

Cost 1s. 6d.

Cut out pattern pieces 27, 28, 29, 30, 31, and 32, Sheet H. Lay out pieces 27, 29, and 31 on double jade green felt, and pieces 32, 28, and 30 on orange felt, as Figs. 77A and 77B (cut out, no turnings required). Cut out, using shapes pattern piece 29 in patterned print. Cut three pieces of print 8½ in by 4½ in., cut three sticks each 6½ in. long for legs and neck, and two 3 in. long for beak. Start making bird by rolling each stick in a strip of print and sewing ends, as Figs. 78A and 78B. Cut out feet, each in two thicknesses of cardboard. Sew covered stick to one. (Fig. 79A.) Make hole in second and thread stick through, so that two thicknesses of cardboard lie one on top of the other with a very small bit of stuffing between. (Fig. 79B.) Cut a hole in one of the foot pieces of orange felt, as shown at *A*, pattern piece 32. Thread this on top of the foot and put the felt without a hole underneath. Tack in place and machine outside of double cardboard. (Fig. 79c.) Machine tail outside of single cardboard. Machine two beak shapes in felt, sharpen two short pieces of stick and push into each beak. Machine

head, leaving beak opening *AB*, pattern piece 31. Put
in eyes, stuff head and insert beaks in opening. Push

PLATE XXV
STICK BIRD

covered stick into opening *C*, pattern piece 31. The
head should look like Fig. 80A. Machine the body
pieces together on right side, allowing $\frac{1}{8}$ in. turning
outside of stitching, leave open between arrows for tail

and stuffing. Push legs up through openings at letter
C on either side of body and head or neck stick down
through opening at *D.* Stuff with Kapox. Join legs and
head together inside body and push tail into opening.
Firmly sew neck, legs, and tail at openings. Fig. 80B
shows body of the bird as if it were transparent, with
legs and neck joined and tail in place. Make and slightly
stuff wings and sew in position as Plate XXV.

MARIONETTE MONKEY. (Plate XXVI.)

Materials—
 ¼ yd. of 36 in. patterned velveteen.
 Two 8 in. squares of yellow felt.
 Ten metal washers.
 Ten wooden washers.
 Some galvanized wire.
 Pair of large animal's eyes.
 Some small pieces of lead or small heavy
  pebbles.
 Piece of fur trimming.
 Some thick black carpet thread.
 Some wooden battens.
 Wood wool for stuffing.   Cost 1s. 8d.

Cut out pattern pieces 33, 34, 35, 36, 37, and 38.
Cut off hands and feet from pattern piece 35. Fold
¼ yd. of patterned material into a double rectangle
18 in. by 9 in., lay out pattern pieces 33, 34, 35, and
36 as Fig. 81A.

Fig. 81B shows (face mask as shown by dotted lines,
pattern piece 34) hands, tail, and ears laid out on double
yellow felt. Cut all these parts out, allowing turnings
on velveteen but no turnings on felt.

PLATE XXVI
MARIONETTE MONKEY

Make hands and feet by machining on right side, slightly stuffing them, machining fingers through stuffing, stuff remainder of hand and sew up opening. The hand should look like Fig. 82A. Machine body, arms, and legs of the monkey and turn right side out, hem hands and feet into bottom of arms and legs, putting a small piece of lead at the bottom when stuffing each limb. The feet should be flat and the hands sideways, as shown in Fig. 83A. Leave tops of limbs open for jointing. Make head in velveteen, inserting gusset at back, so that letters *AB*, pattern pieces 34 and 36, match. Make face mask in yellow felt, put in eyes and embroider mouth and nose (position shown on pattern piece 34). The face looks more grotesque if the eyelids are cut out in yellow felt and put on over the eyes. (Fig. 82B.) Put on face mask over velveteen, after the head is stuffed, then hem on dotted line, pattern piece 34. Sew on a piece of narrow fur trimming to cover join. Make ears and sew on as marked, pattern piece 34.

The monkey is put together with joints and wires, and its limbs and head are attached by carpet thread strings to short wooden batons, so that by working these up and down the monkey will dance. Fig. 83A shows the wires and washers in position, the joints have to be put in as the toy is stuffed. This was described for William goat earlier in this chapter. The only difference being that in the leg joints of the goat each leg had a separate wire, and in this monkey a wire passes right through from side to side of the body. Fig. 83B shows three lengths of wood cut and the monkey strung up on carpet thread (dotted lines represent thread), so that by holding the batten in the

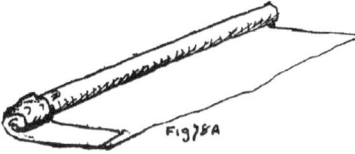

Fig 78 A

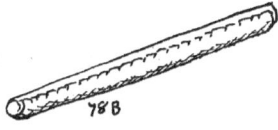

78 B

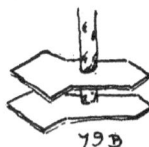

79 B

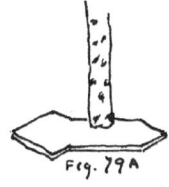

Fig. 79 A

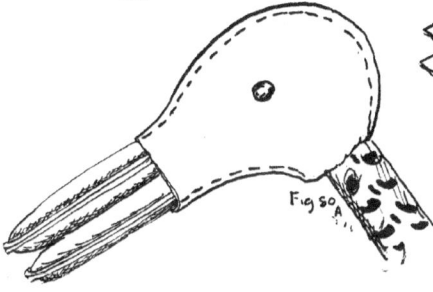

Fig 80 A

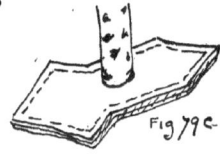

Fig 79 C

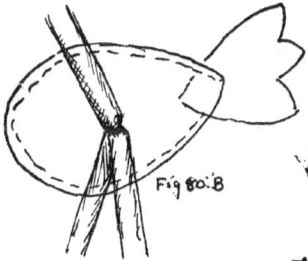

Fig 80 B

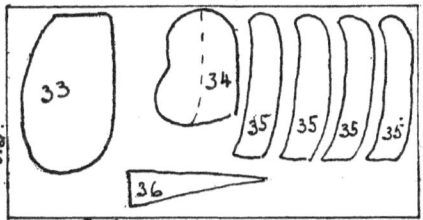

Fold

33

34

35 35 35 35

36

Fig 81 A

82 A.

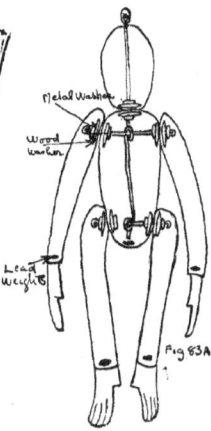

Metal Washer
Wood Washer
Lead Weights
Fig 83A

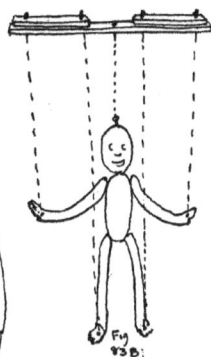

Fig 83 B

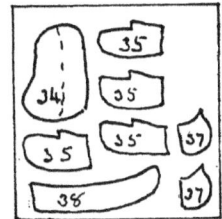

34

35

35

35

35

37

38

37

Fig 81 B

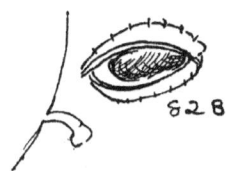

82 B

right hand, with the second finger under the centre of the batten, and the first and third fingers between the long and short battens on either side, by working the fingers up and down the monkey will dance in the most amusing way.

CHAPTER VIII

BOUDOIR OR SOFA DOLLS

A dancing shape, an image gay.
To haunt, to startle, and way-lay.
WORDSWORTH.

In this chapter three of these charming toys are described. It is felt that there is no need to give patterns either of the dolls or their clothing, as they are exactly the same in construction as those described in Chapter V. The only difference being in proportion, so the measurements will be given. The clothing also will be described, but no patterns given; after following the patterns in Chapter V the toy-maker should have no difficulty in cutting whatever garment she desires.

Miss Japanese (Plate XXVII) is 20 in. long with very slender body and limbs, short square feet, and rather a long oval face. Method of making as doll "Josephine," Chapter V. Her hair is made of black rug wool coiled in the Japanese style and decorated with artificial daisies, which give the appearance of chrysanthemums. Her face is painted and can easily be followed from Plate XXVII.

She wears loose yellow sateen trousers with pink stripes applied $\frac{1}{2}$ in. up from bottom of legs, black square shoes of sateen, a kimono of gaily-patterned cotton crepe, pink, blue, and black bound with pink, and a wide royal blue belt or sash tied in a broad bow at the back.

Susanne (Plate XXVIII) is 23 in. long, cut much as

PLATE XXVII
MISS JAPANESE

PLATE XXVIII
SUSANNE

Miss Japanese, but with smaller head, longer legs, and very slender, pointed feet.

Hair of white sheep's wool arranged in a long bob with a band of black ribbon. Susanne wears white silk knickers and a pierrette's dress with tight black satin bodice and pale green organdi frills, four at the skirt and three at the neck, picot edged with black. She wears black ribbon bows at her wrists, and black satin shoes kept on with crossed black ribbons up the legs. Painted doll-like face with blue eyes.

BELINDA (Plate XXIX) is 28 in. long. Her legs are 15 in. and her arms 12 in. from shoulder to finger tips. Miss Japanese and Susanne both had bent arms, but Belinda's arms are quite straight and she is very slender—her body is shaped in to a small waist.

She wears yellow organdi knickers and a plain yellow organdi skirt right down to her feet, then a skirt of frilled spotted white net. These frilled nets can be bought quite cheaply all made up ready for children's frocks. This white skirt is 18 in. long and 1¼ yd. around the bottom. The dress is pale blue net. The skirt has six pleated frills edged with silver (also bought made up by the yard). The bodice is a cross-over affair with short sleeves and a black rosette at the waist in front. The skirt is gathered tight to the waist. Over this dress Belinda wears a fairly tight-fitting evening coat of blue velveteen edged with white fur. She has a necklace of two rows of pearls graded in size from tiny ones at the back to quite large ones in front. She wears shoes of black felt with high heels formed of rolls of felt and a pearl on each toe. Her hair is white sheep's wool, arranged in two small coils behind each ear, and her face is painted.

PLATE XXIX
BELINDA

Belinda is a really beautiful doll, and no one seeing her for the first time would believe that she was made of cheap underclothing material. It is dolls of this type that should prove so useful to students and others interested in dress design.

* 9 7 8 1 4 7 3 3 3 6 3 1 5 *